A POCKET GUIDE TO SKETCHING

Ray Evans

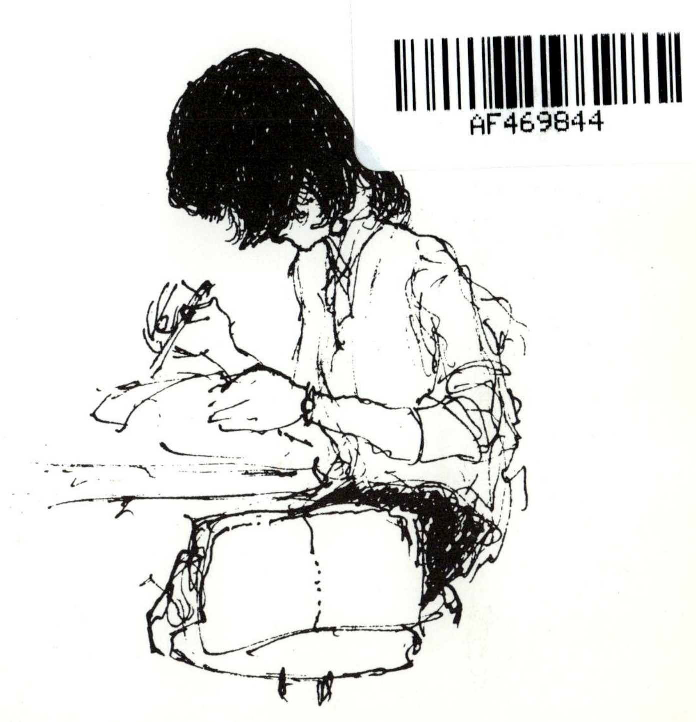

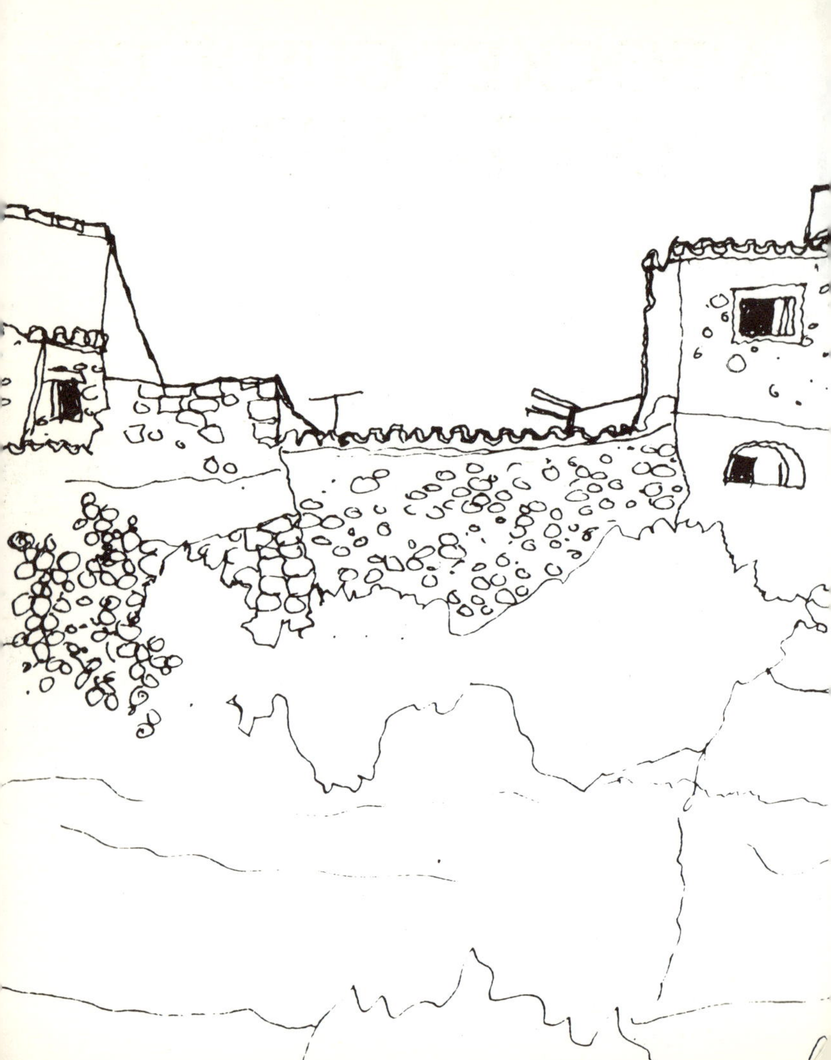

A POCKET GUIDE TO SKETCHING

Ray Evans

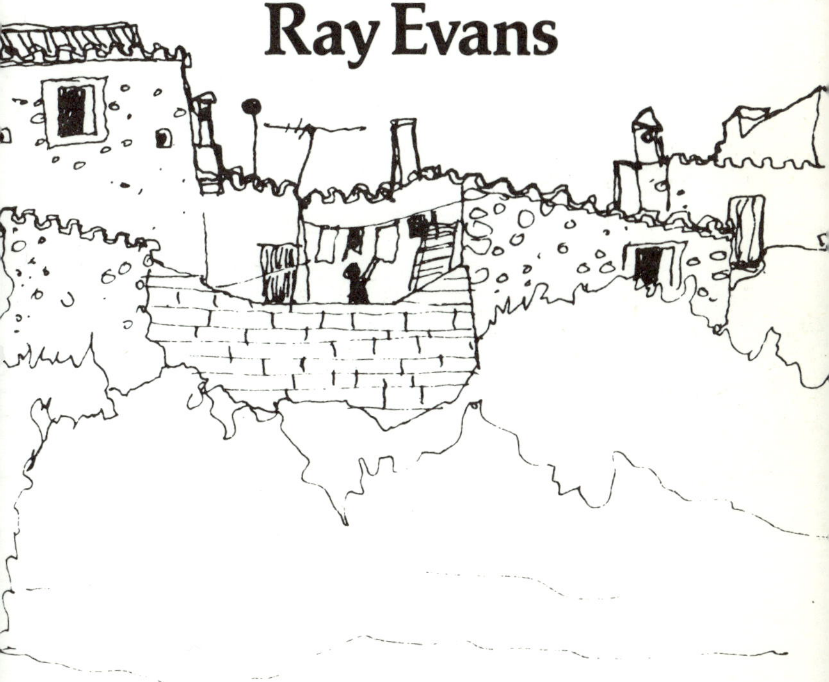

COLLINS

First published in 1986
by William Collins Sons & Co Ltd
London · Glasgow · Sydney
Auckland · Johannesburg

Designed by Caroline Hill

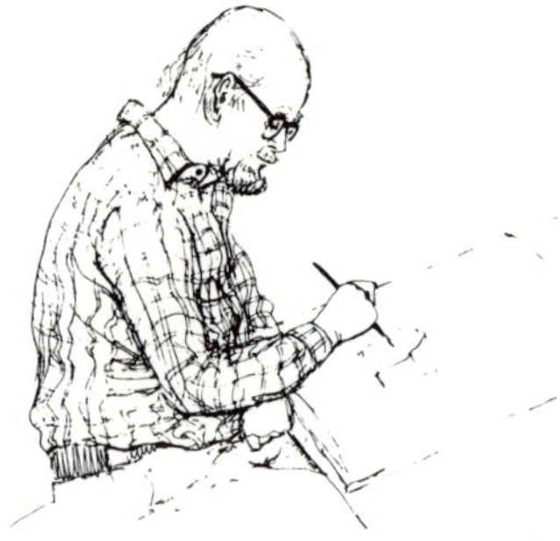

British Library Cataloguing in Publication Data

Evans, Ray
Pocket guide to sketching
1. Drawing
I. Title
741.2 NC710
ISBN 0 00 411991 6

Typeset by Centracet
Printed in Spain by
Graficas Reunidas, Madrid

CONTENTS

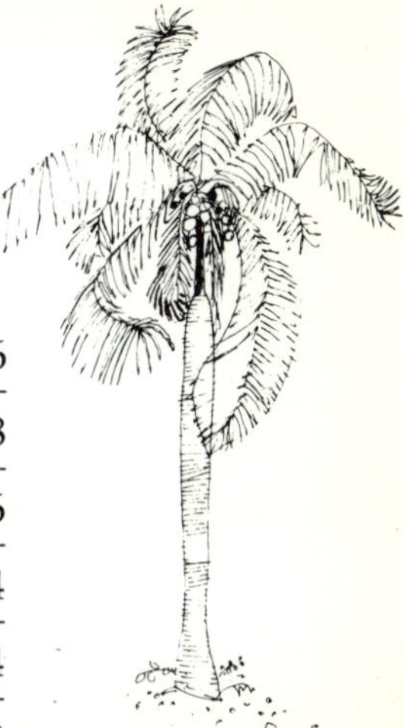

Coconut tree, Thailand: technical pen, 6 × 3½ in (152 × 90 mm)

OPPOSITE
Ray by Angela: felt pen, 7 × 5 in (118 × 140 mm)

INTRODUCTION

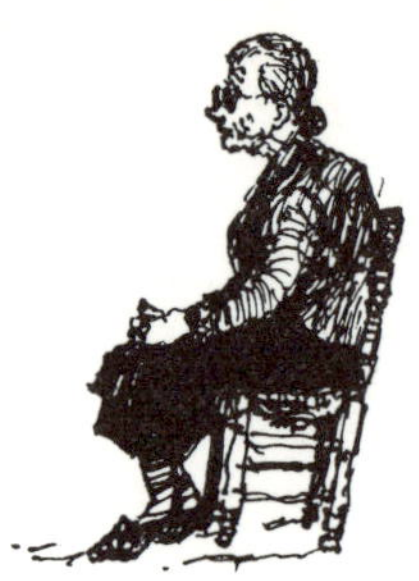

Old lady, Spain: fountain pen, S/S

A sketchbook serves many purposes for an artist but after a lifetime of using a variety of sketchbooks I have come to the conclusion that a 'pocket sketchbook' has its own very special function.

The traditional larger-sized artist's sketchbook is more often used for making studies in the field to finish off as paintings in the studio, or for making drawings or watercolours that are an end in themselves. Whereas I carry my pocket sketchbook absolutely everwhere with me so that I have it to hand ready to be used when and where the opportunity arises. In fact, I feel quite undressed without it!

We all spend a great deal of time waiting around when travelling to and from work, or on holiday – in buses, trains, airports and stations – and these moments should not be wasted.

Street cleaner, Bangkok: technical pen, 2 × 2 in (50 × 50 mm)

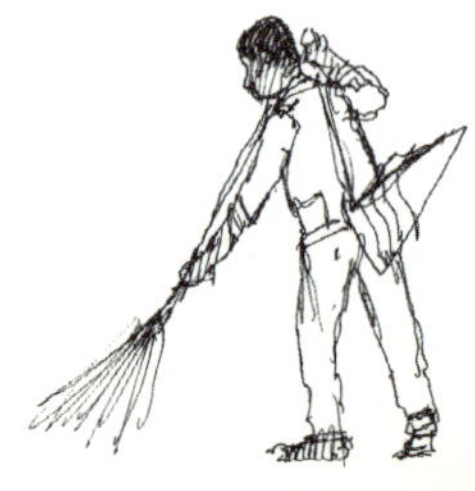

Moreover, they often provide a rich source of the variety and spice of life and some good subjects for sketching.

Problems such as composition and perspective for a painting are best worked out in the pocket sketchbook and in addition it comes into its own for me as a way of recording notes, ideas and thoughts about the subjects one is sketching. In fact, it becomes an illustrated sketchbook diary. And above all, it is a source of observation, learning and, of course, enjoyment.

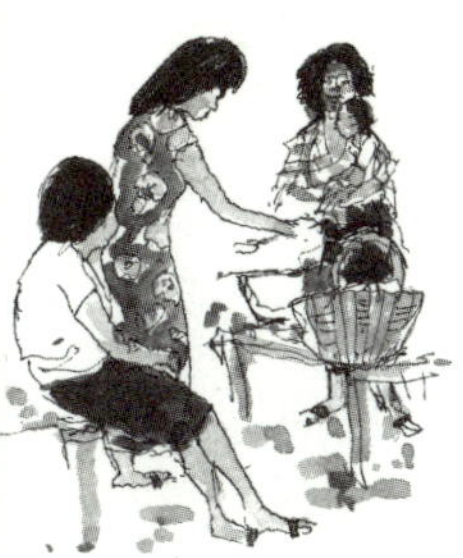

Street scene, Thailand: pen and watercolour, 2½ × 2½ in (60 × 60 mm)

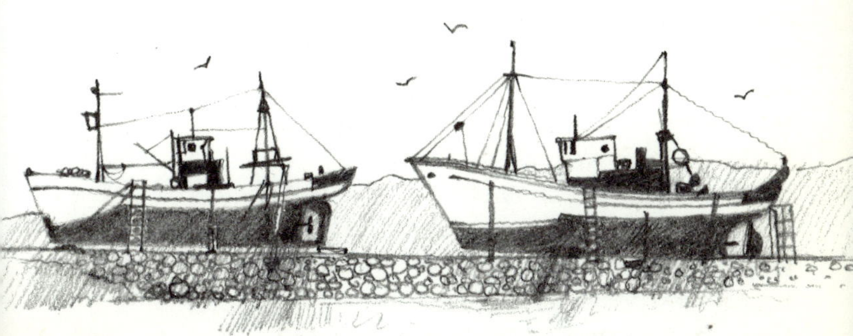

Fishing boats, Garrucha, Spain: B pencil, S/S

EQUIPMENT AND MATERIALS

On the next few pages I have listed and illustrated, with the marks they make, a number of different drawing tools. However, the choice of drawing instruments today is enormous and their quality is improving all the time. It is up to you, therefore, to experiment and after a time you will decide on the ones that you find the most suitable for your style of drawing.

The points to look out for with pens are whether they are easy to use, whether the ink is waterproof or not and whether it flows easily, and if the pen gives you the thickness or thinness of line you want. Pencils also come in different strengths so choose the ones you feel happiest with. I find that the Kolinsky Diana range of sable brushes are the best but they are expensive, whereas the Dalon synthetic brushes are much cheaper and

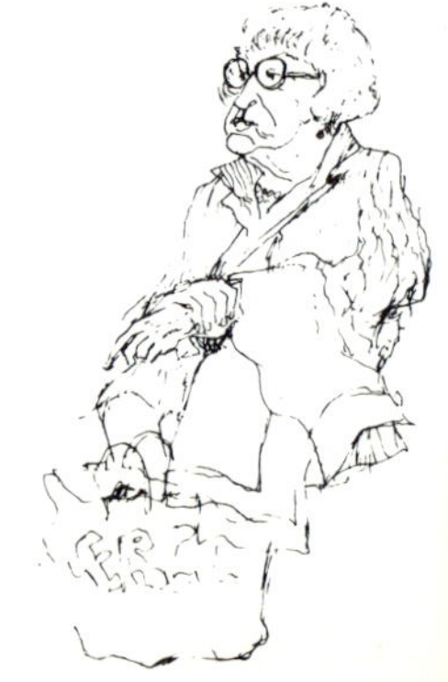

'Lady in waiting' at St Louis Airport, USA: technical pen, 4½ × 3 in (115 × 77 mm)

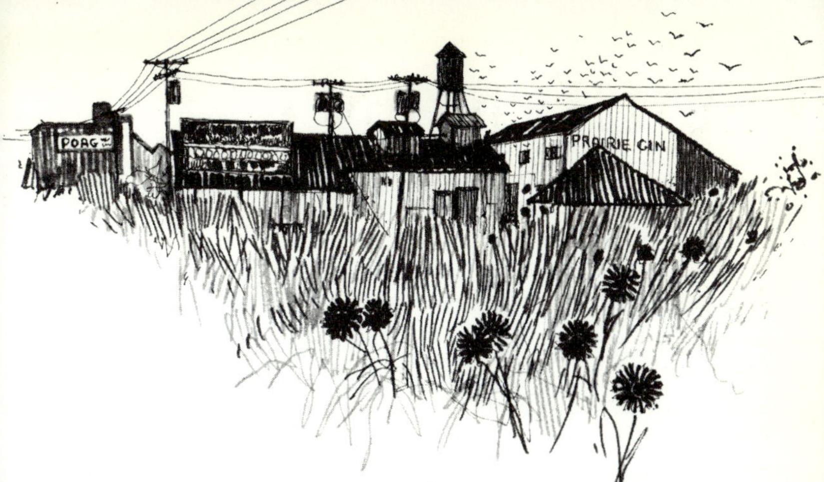

Prairie Gin, Chickasha, USA: coloured felt pens, 7 × 4½ in (178 × 114 mm)

a good substitute if you cannot afford sable. Your brushes should be washed carefully after use, especially if they have been used for ink washes.

I tend to limit myself to a few basic colours when using watercolours for sketching and my basic kit would comprise: Prussian Blue, Raw Sienna, Gamboge, Brown Madder, Cadmium Red and Black. If I had room for more then I would add: Cobalt Blue, Alizarin or Venetian Red, Burnt Sienna, Raw Umber, Sap Green, Ivory Black and Chinese White. I find that the Rowney watercolours are excellent, especially their Artists' Quality range.

Pens

Here is a selection of my favourite pens. Try to look after your pens and do not leave the caps off, or they will quickly dry out.

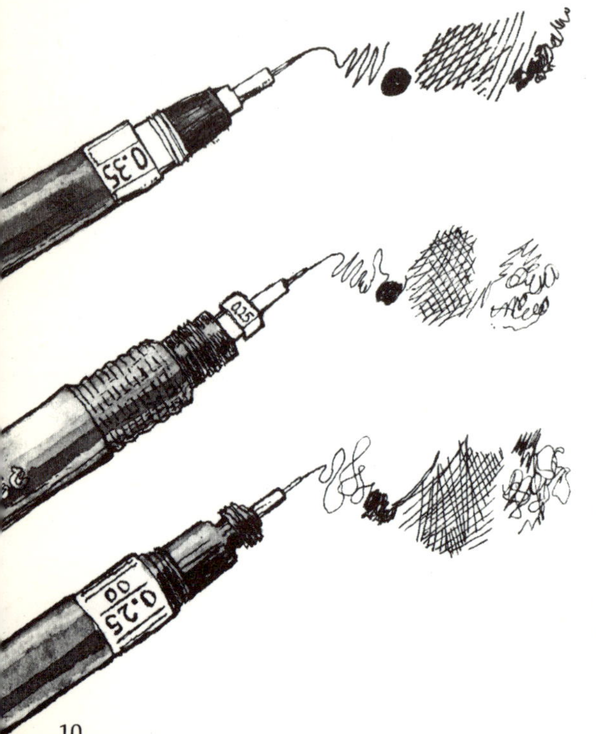

The Rotring 2000 0.35 Isograph architect's technical pen. Uses its own special waterproof ink. Keep clean and make sure the cap is firmly in place when not in use.

Staedtler Marsmatic 700 0.25. This is similar to the Rotring.

TG1. S Faber-Castell. Also similar to the Rotring but has a moist cap fitting over the nib.

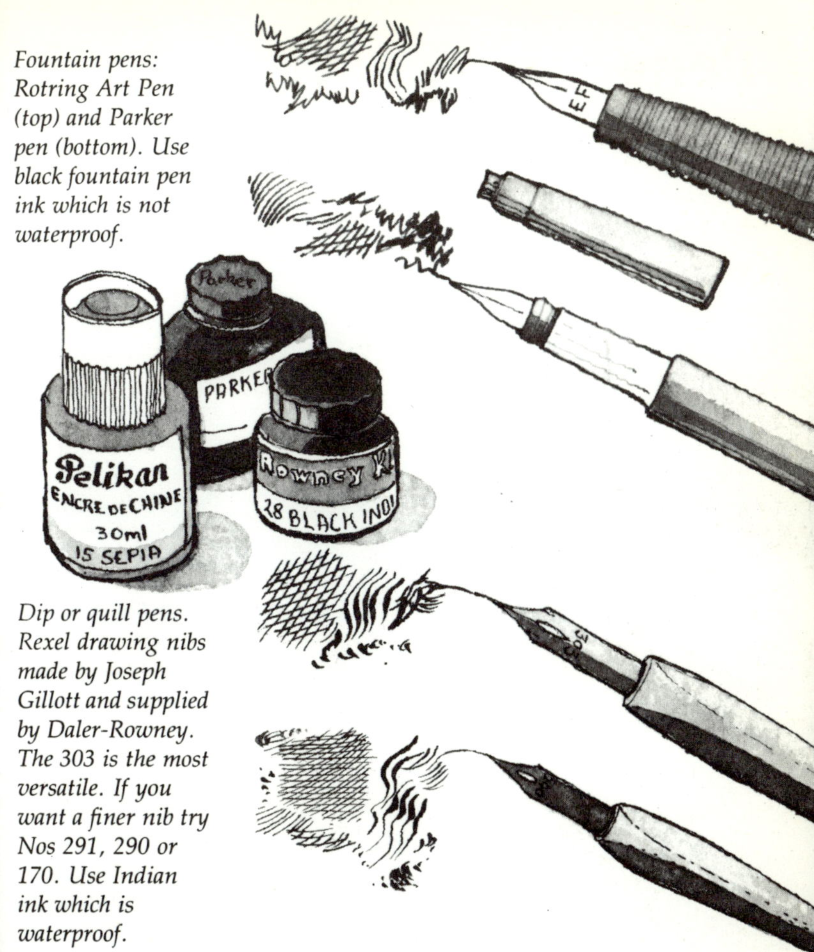

Fountain pens: Rotring Art Pen (top) and Parker pen (bottom). Use black fountain pen ink which is not waterproof.

Dip or quill pens. Rexel drawing nibs made by Joseph Gillott and supplied by Daler-Rowney. The 303 is the most versatile. If you want a finer nib try Nos 291, 290 or 170. Use Indian ink which is waterproof.

In my opinion, water-based felt or fibre tipped pens are the best for colour sketching work. The ink from all these colour pens, however, will fade in strong sunlight, as will watercolours, although some pens, like the Fibralo, are more light-fast than others.

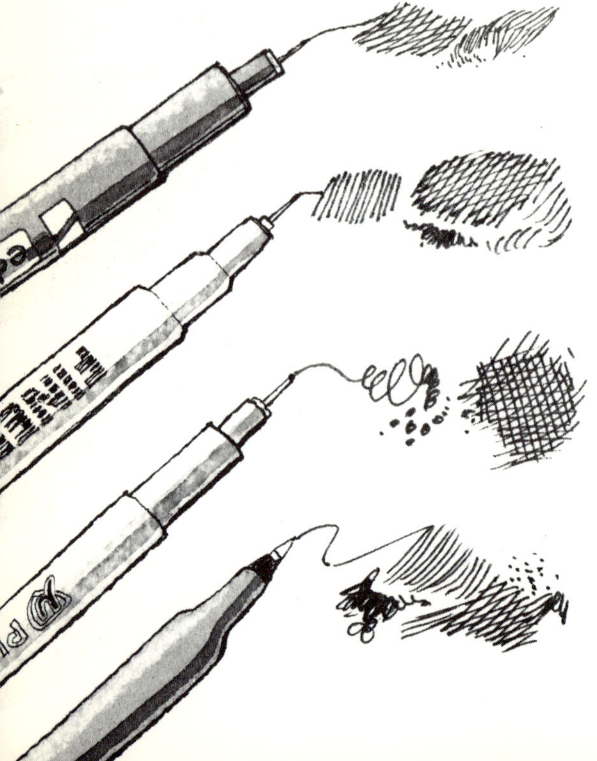

Edding 1800 Point 0.1. Fine point but not waterproof.

Finepoint System pens. Variety of thicknesses, not waterproof.

Pygma. Variety of thicknesses of nib;waterproof.

Pentel Super Ball. Fine line ballpoint, not waterproof.

Tombo 0.25. Variety of thicknesses, not waterproof.

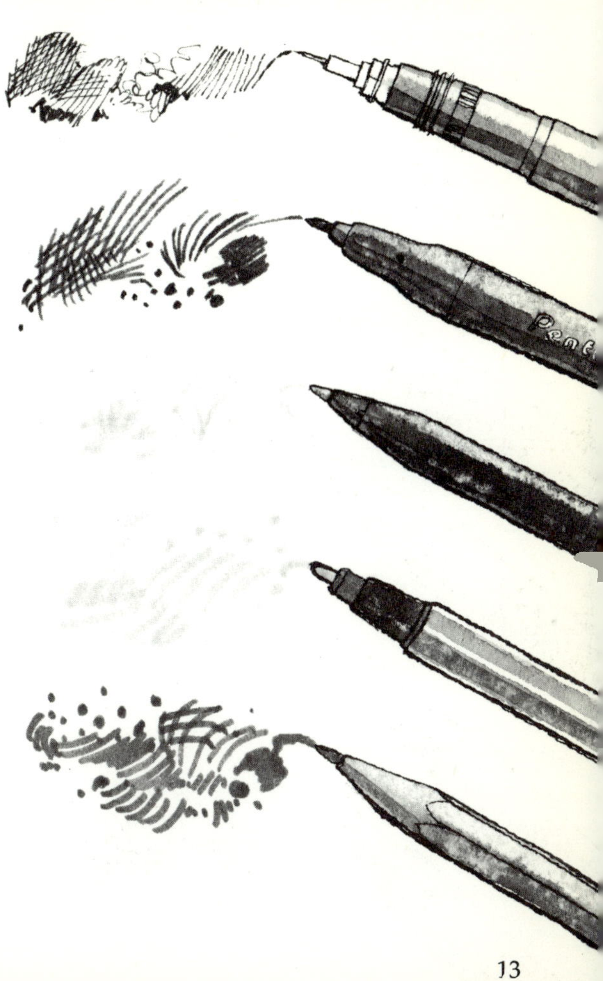

Pentel Color pen. Fine point, strong water-based colours.

Edding 1200 Color pen, fine line.

Stabilo Colour pen.

Fibralo, Caran D'Ache. Good strong colours that do not fade easily.

Mixed Media

With colour pens I tend to use the pastel colours of browny-grey, blue-grey and ochre, but with crayons or watercolour pencils I go for stronger, more vibrant colours. I prefer watercolours in tubes but there are also some good miniature watercolour boxes with pans.

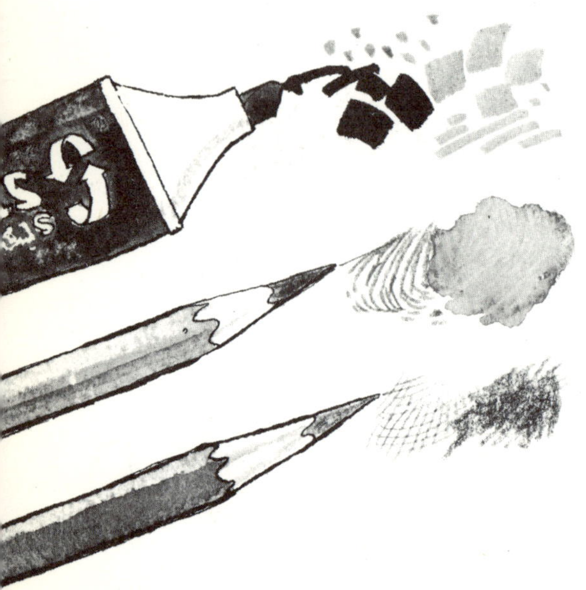

Stabilayout. Colour water-based pen for broader work, chisel point allows for a variety of line.

Derwent watercolour pencils. Smooth to use, but give an effect rather like pastels.

Berol Prismacolor. Good strong crayon colours.

Rowney Victoria pencils and crayons. Good colour range.

Rowney Kolinsky Diana round brushes, series 40. The finest sable for watercolour, but expensive.

Dalon series D77 round watercolour brush, much cheaper than the sable.

Dalon series D44 for square brush techniques.

The Rowney Artists' Watercolour Box. Excellent for travelling. Contains 12 watercolours, a sable brush and water reservoir, 3½ × 2½ in (90 × 60 mm).

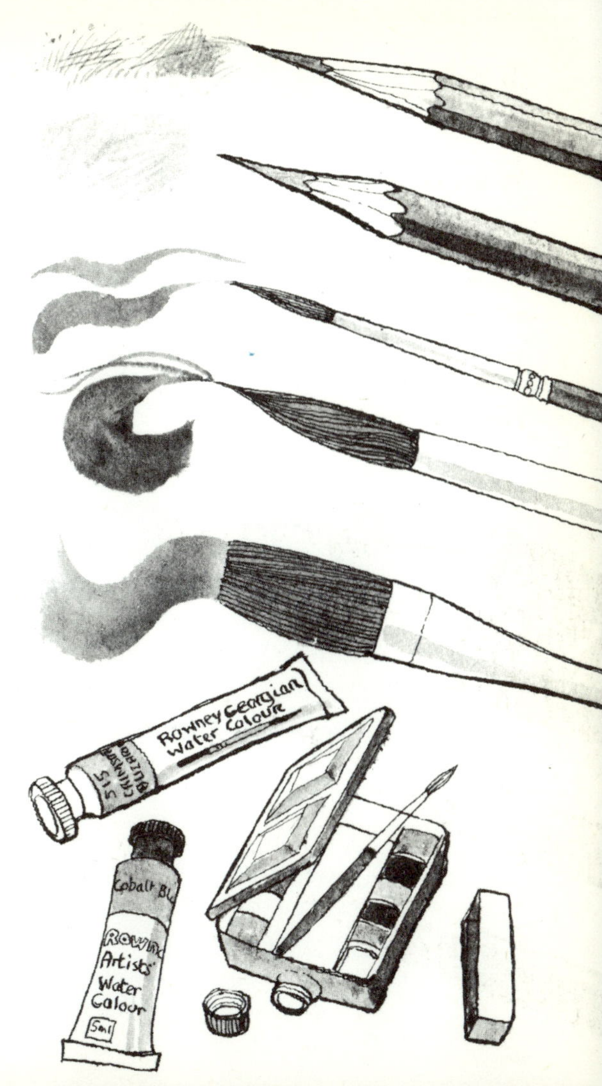

SKETCHING TECHNIQUES

When going out sketching always take the drawing instruments that you have found give you the best results and are easiest to use. Do not try to take a whole range of tools with you but just select a few you are happiest with. However, it is good to ring the changes occasionally with different materials, perhaps by adding a coloured wash or colour pencil to an otherwise monochrome subject. By experimenting in this way you will gradually become familiar with a variety of drawing instruments.

OPPOSITE
The Alhambra, Granada, Spain: Berol Prismacolor crayons, S/S. These fine crayons were ideal for portraying the delicate winter light.

Fishing boats, Garrucha, Spain: technical pen and wash $5\frac{3}{4} \times 1\frac{1}{4}$ in (148 × 32 mm)

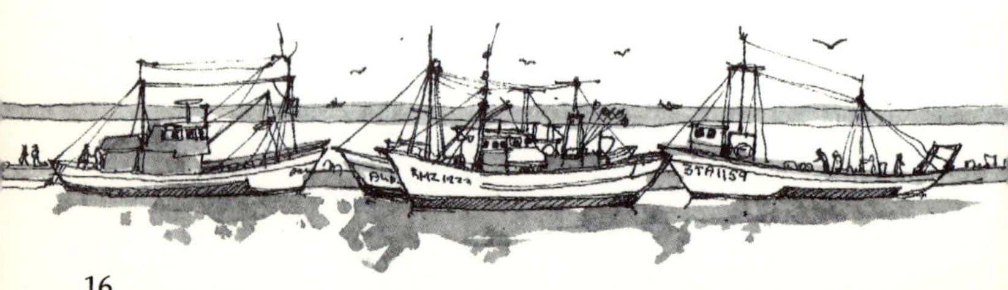

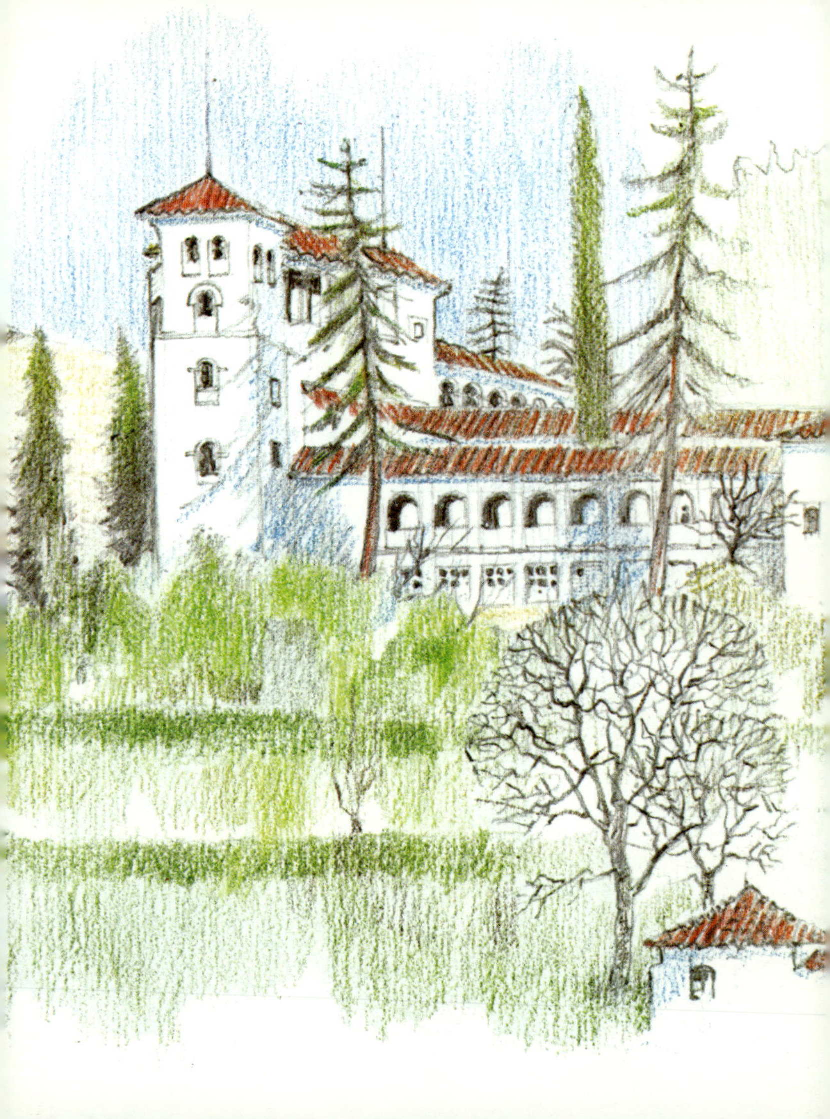

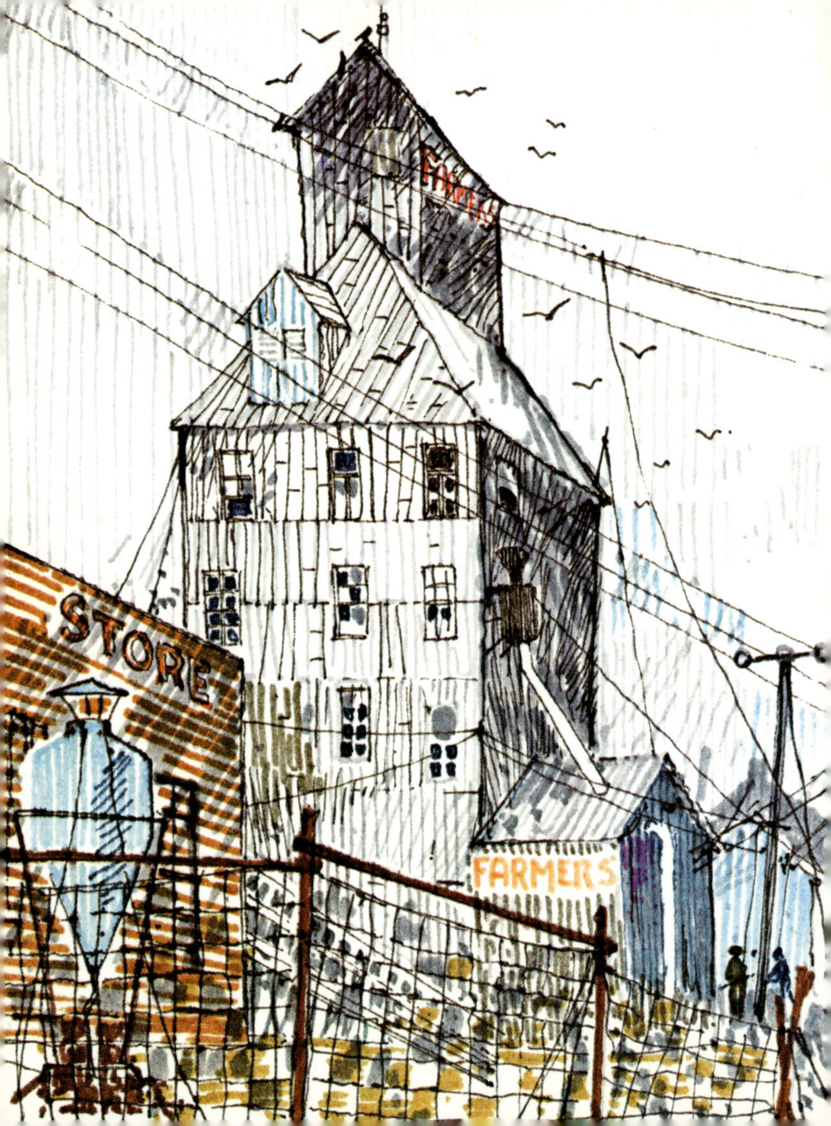

STORE
FARMERS'

OPPOSITE *Flour Mill, Oklahoma, USA: coloured felt pens, s/s. The harshness of the industrial buildings needed the bolder colour of felt pens.*

In normal everyday travelling, I like to carry only the minimum of sketching equipment: an architect's technical pen and a favourite fountain pen, both fully charged with ink, and my pocket sketchbook. If my journey is of a more leisurely nature I add my Rowney 12B Artists' Watercolour Box as illustrated on page 15. I am then fully primed to carry out most of the work shown in this book.

However, if I am going on a long trip or holiday, then I take part of my studio with me in a lightweight sketching bag large enough to take a 14 × 10 in (355 × 255 mm) sketch pad. I have described my sketching bag in more detail on page 112. With this bag you can extend your range of sketchbooks and carry blotting paper (useful for giving texture and speeding up work), a larger watercolour box, water pot, pencils, brushes, fibre tipped pens, quill pens, a knife and Indian ink.

The majority of the sketches in this book have been reproduced actual size and are from small pocket sketchbooks like the Daler-Rowney Series 42, size 5¼ × 4 in (134 × 100 mm), which contain a smooth sketching paper suitable for pen, pen and wash, watercolour, pencil or fibre tipped pens on this scale. If I am using a larger sketchbook then I like them with a watercolour paper (see page 114).

Because most of the drawings are reproduced same size you can see the details and techniques used more easily. This has not been possible in every case but where there is a reduction in size then the actual size of the drawing has been noted in the caption, with the vertical measurement first. When the sketch has been reproduced virtually the same size as my original, then I have labelled it S/S.

Many of the small sketches in this section stand on their own and do not need much explanation but I would like to enlarge a bit on the technique I used when I drew the fishing boat opposite. This beautifully shaped boat was pulled up on the beach and I decided to draw it from a rather difficult position – practically head on, so

Fishing boat, Garrucha, Spain: Staedtler technical pen 0.25, 6 × 5 in (152 × 128 mm)

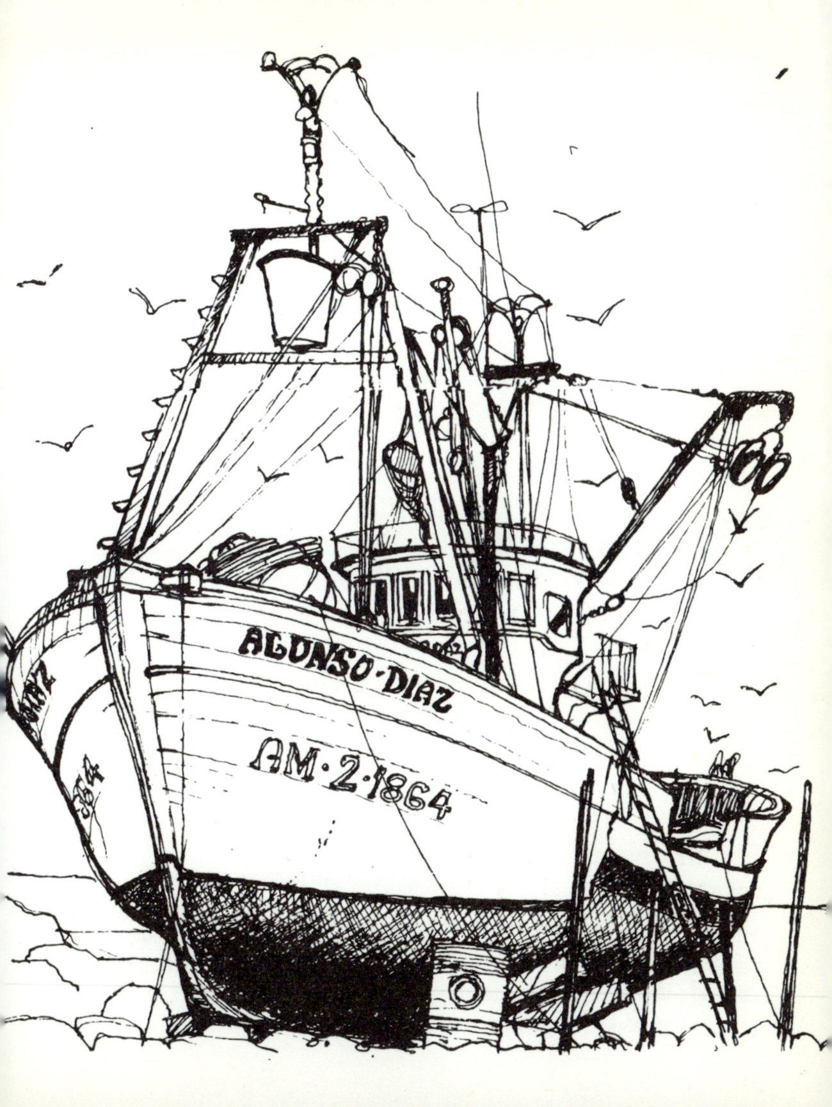
ALONSO-DIAZ
AM-2-1864

that the whole boat appeared very much foreshortened. I drew across two pages of my small sketchbook with a technical pen and suddenly realized that I wasn't going to get it on to the two pages, nor had I got the shape of the hull right. Second time round it came out better. You will see that I used the technique of cross-hatching on the base of the boat instead of solid black.

OPPOSITE *Tuk-Tuk, Bangkok: Edding fibre tipped pen,* S/S

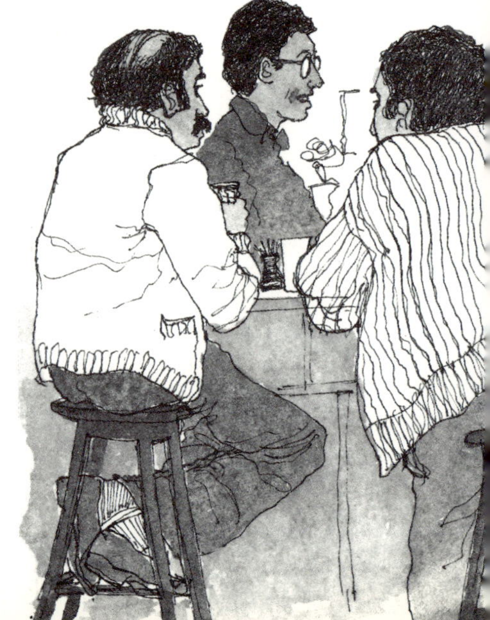

Bar in Spain: technical pen and wash, 5 × 4 in (128 × 100 mm)

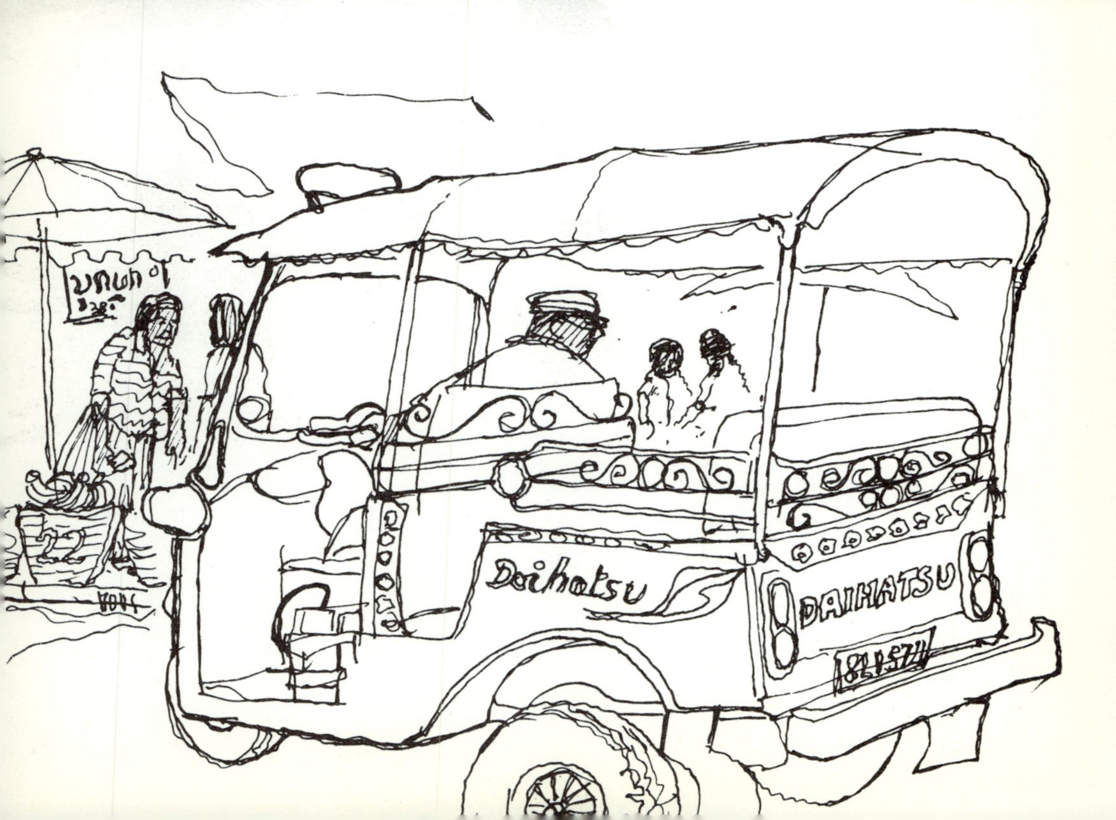
Daihatsu
DAIHATSU

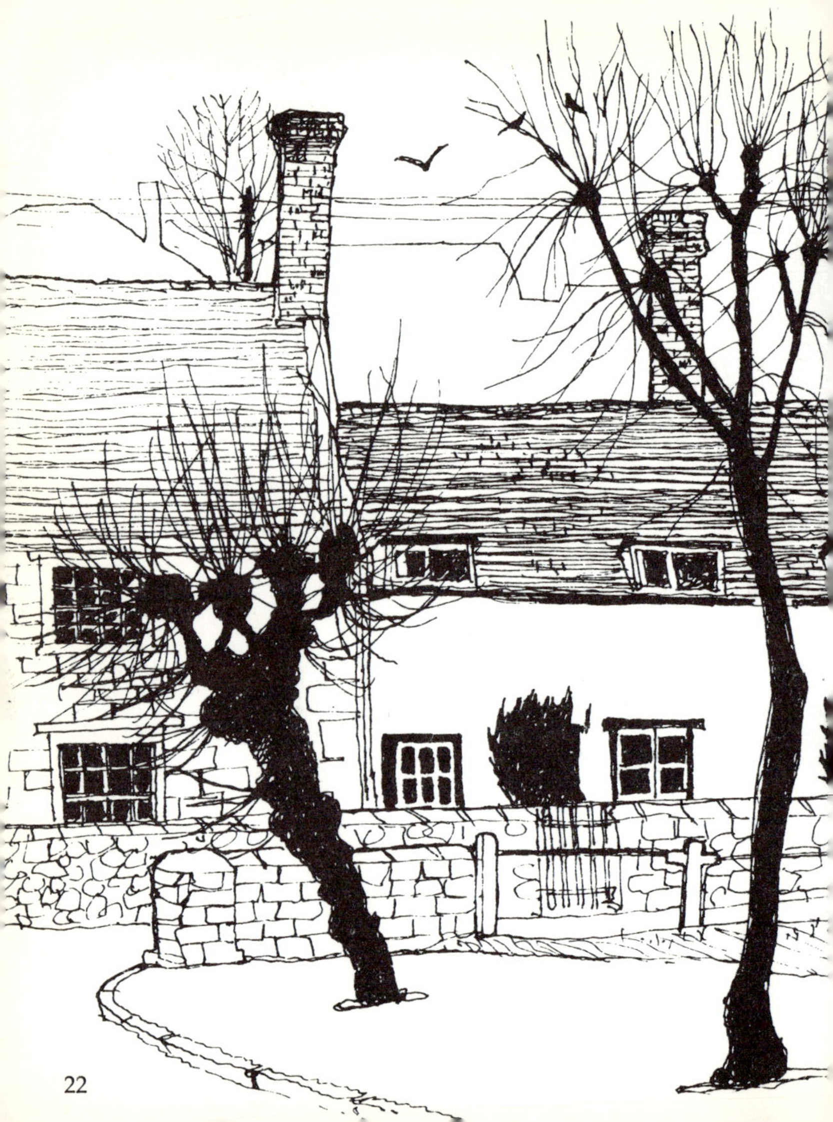

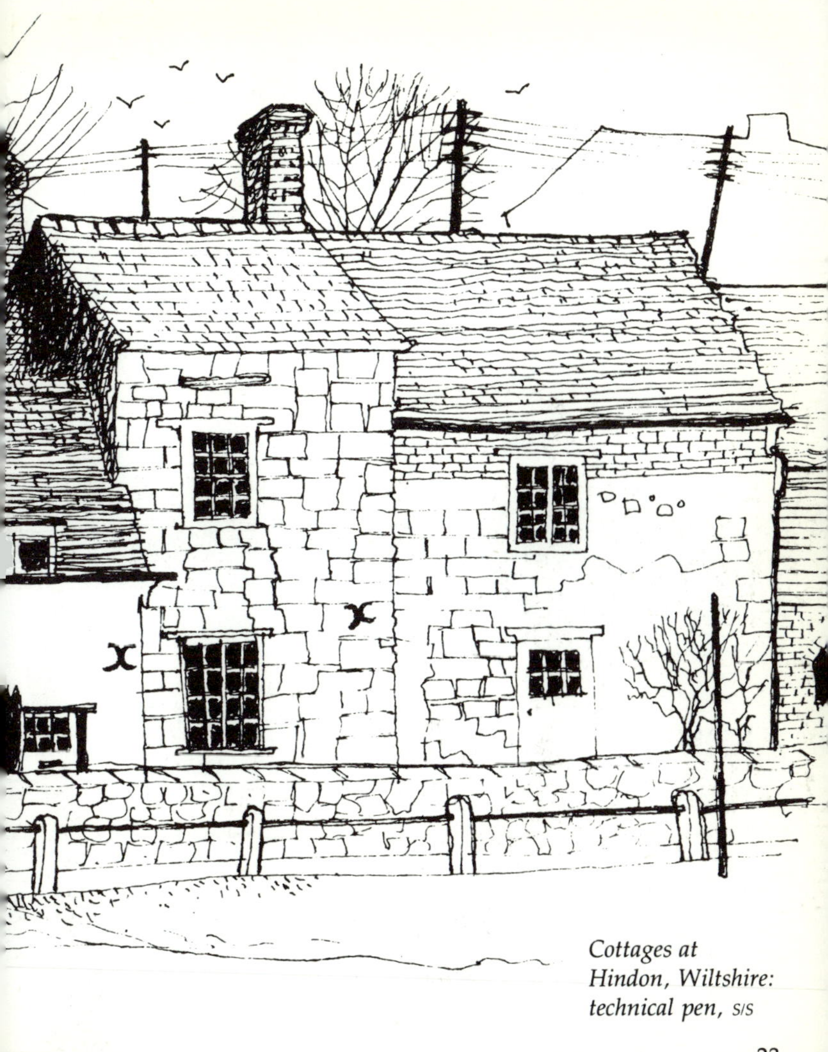

Cottages at Hindon, Wiltshire: technical pen, S/S

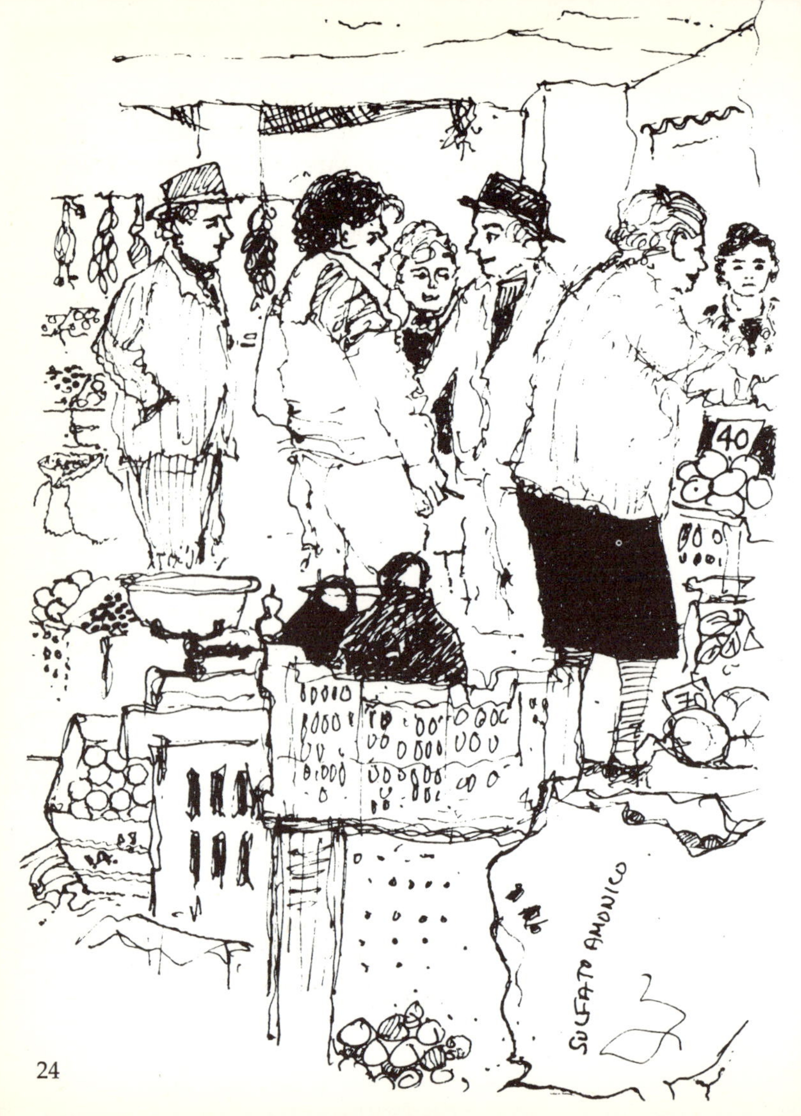
40
SULFATO AMONICO

OPPOSITE *Garrucha Market, Spain: technical pen,* S/S

I became so absorbed with the new drawing that it was not until I was walking home later with a friend who asked to see the drawing, that I realized that I had not even looked at the completed thing myself! This may seem an odd thing to say, but in fact I get so completely absorbed in the subject when I am drawing, and not in the technique, that I often do not look at it as a complete drawing.

This brings me to another point: I deliberately change my drawing instruments and techniques from time to time as it is a useful exercise to try occasionally. For example, when I am drawing with reproduction in mind I design my work much more (see pages 22 and 23). Although I drew this scene with the same technical pen that I used for the boat on page 19, and I

Tea lady, Bangkok: technical pen, S/S

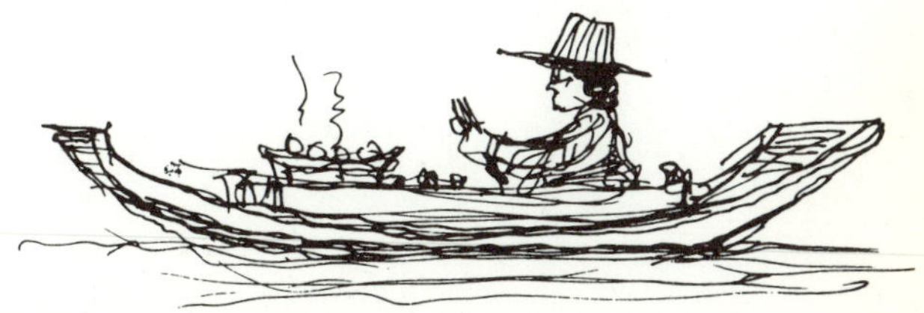

OPPOSITE
Carboneras, Spain: technical pen and wash, S/S

drew it on the spot, I designed the drawing to make use of areas of solid black and different tonal values to make different patterns and shapes. So, do not be afraid to introduce the occasional area of solid black into your sketches to enhance the composition and to emphasize distance. If you are afraid of spoiling a sketch then a piece of paper can be coloured black and the shape cut out and placed over the area on your drawing to see the effect.

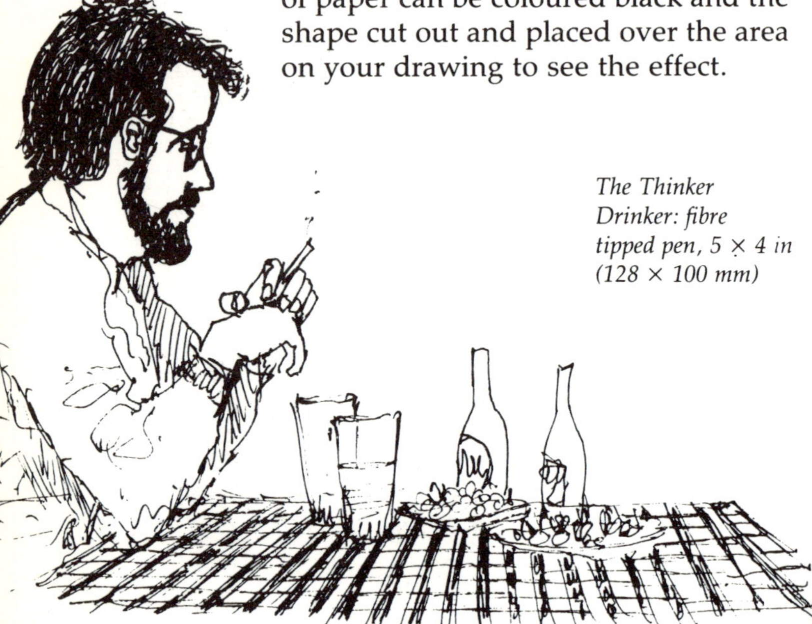

The Thinker Drinker: fibre tipped pen, 5 × 4 in (128 × 100 mm)

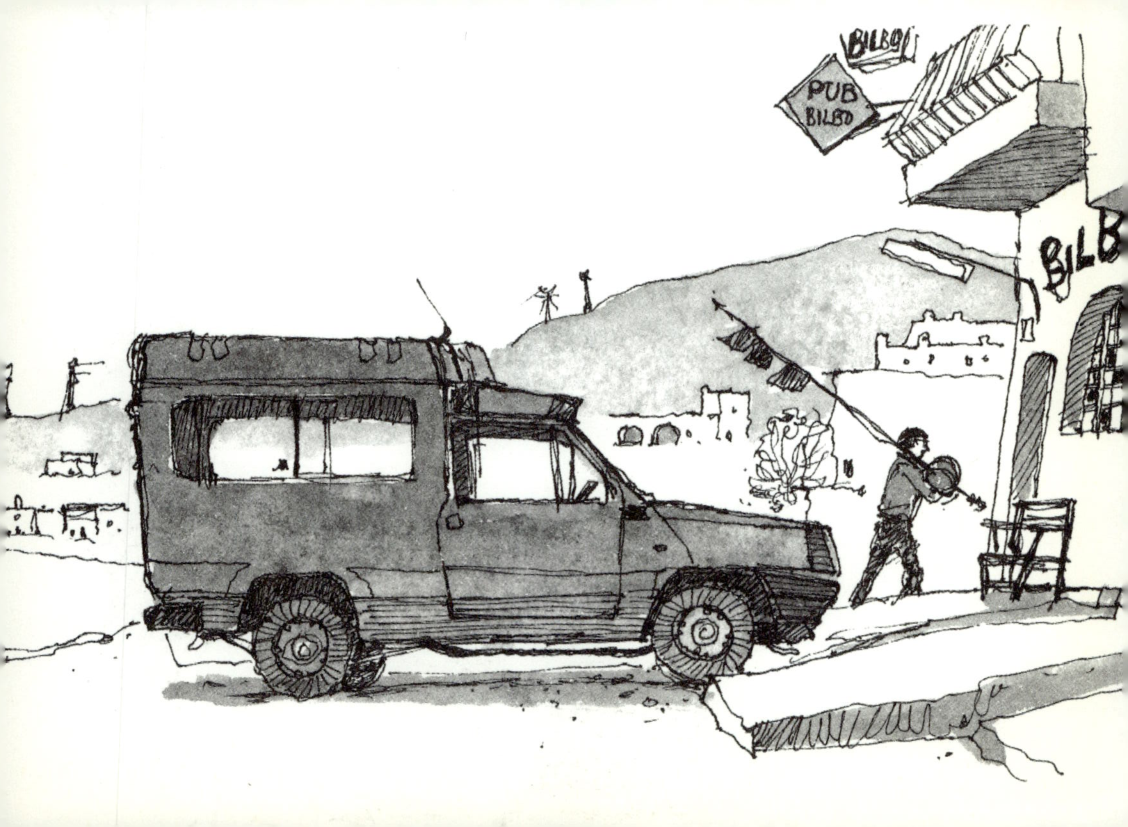
BILBO
PUB
BILBO
BILB

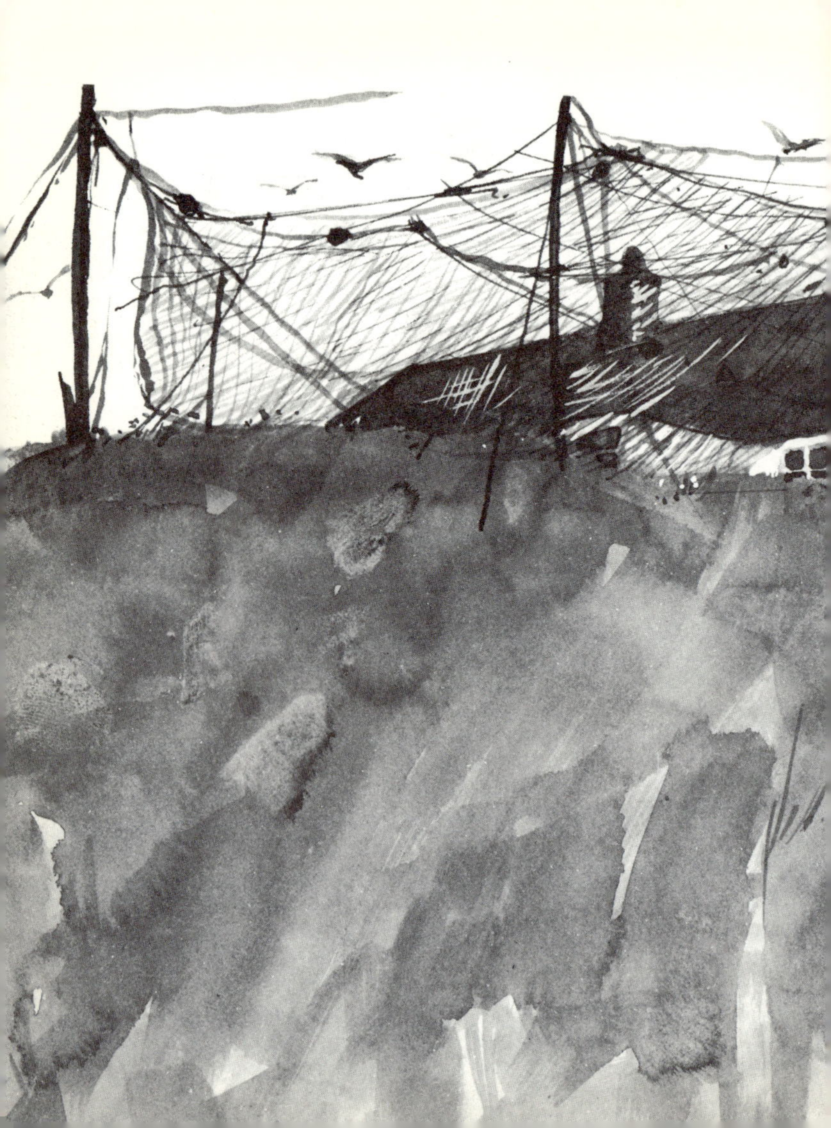

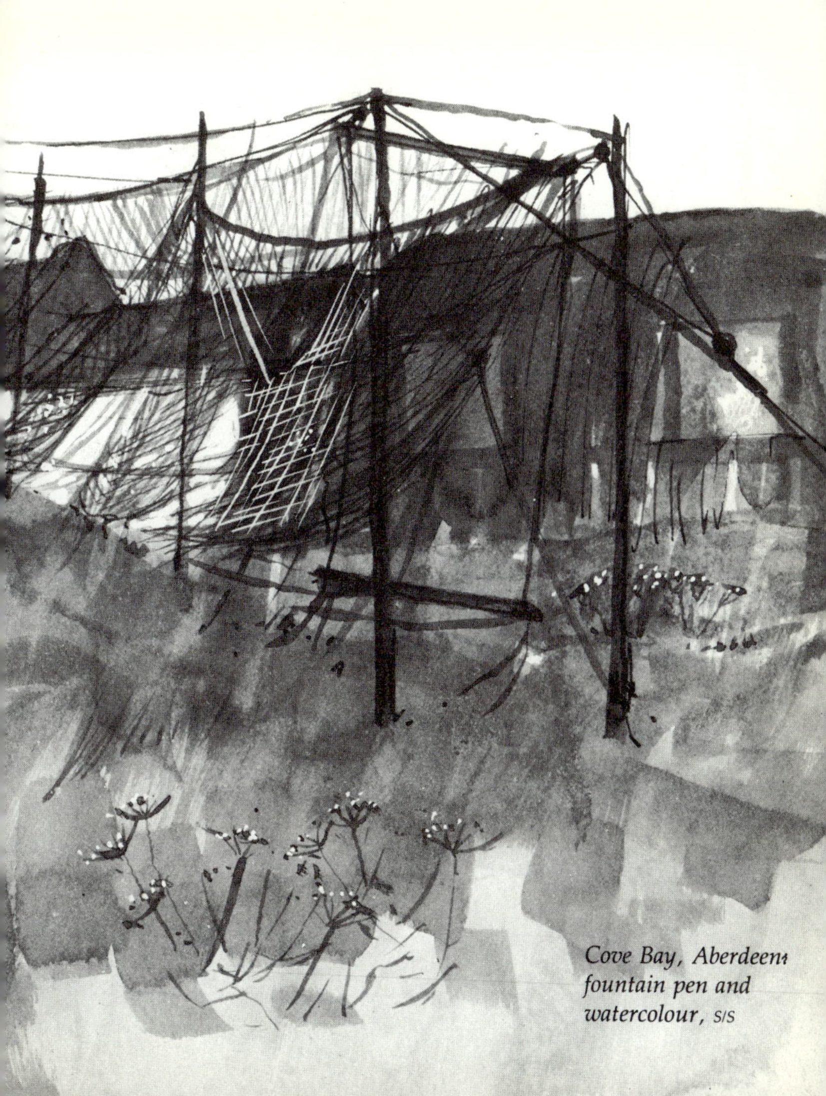

Cove Bay, Aberdeen:
fountain pen and
watercolour, S/S

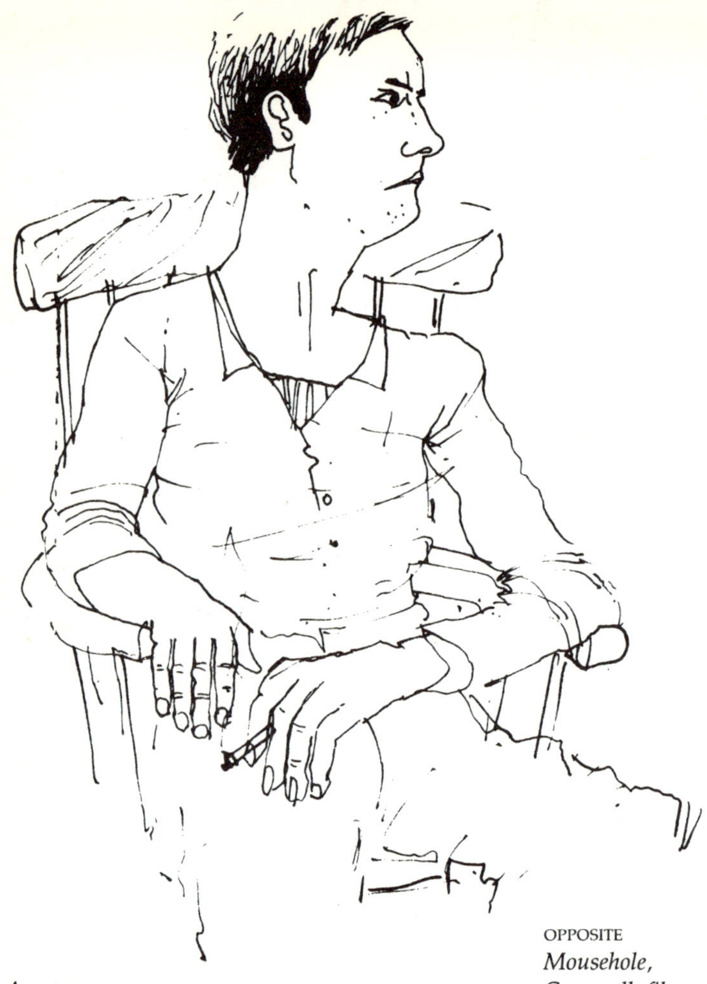

Angry young man: technical pen, S/S

OPPOSITE
Mousehole, Cornwall: fibre tipped pen, S/S

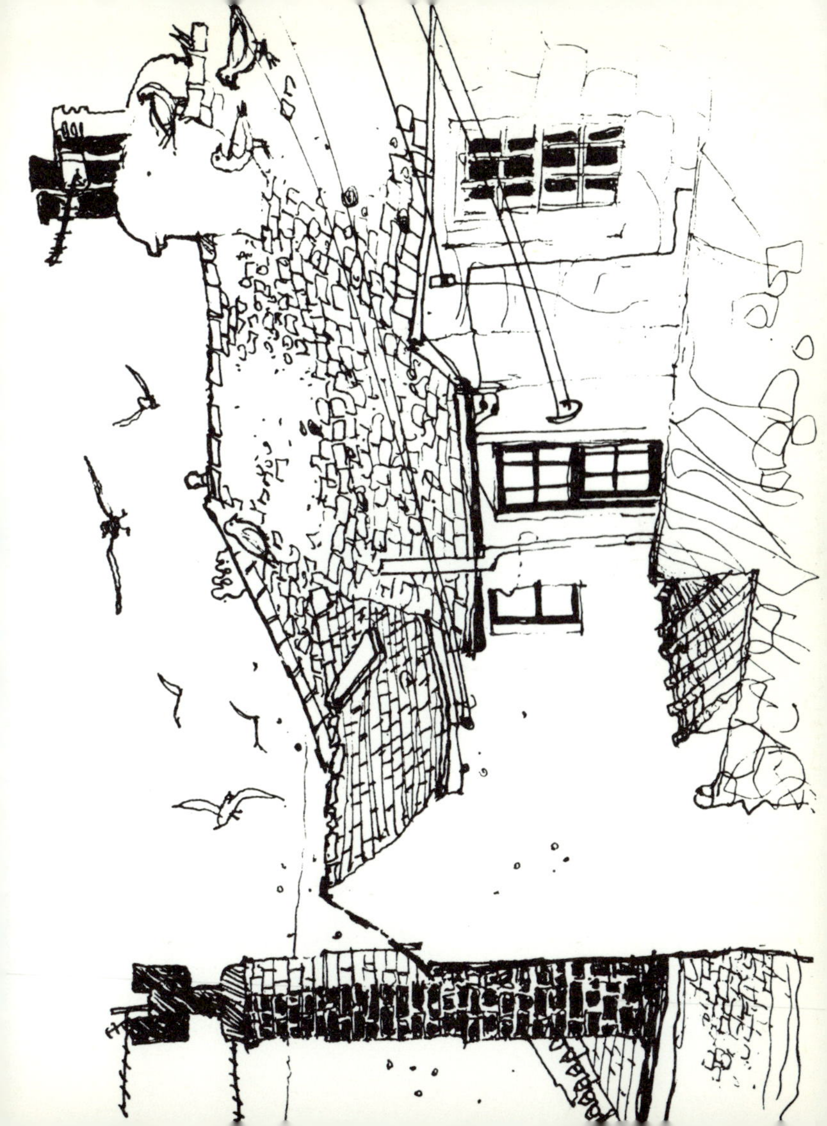

All the time you are drawing in a sketchbook you are learning and observing. Try experimenting by pushing a drawing further than you usually go, or by approaching it in a different way. It is exciting to try out different techniques like cross-hatching or using tonal areas, either with solid black or with a paler wash, as well as the more usual linear approach.

OPPOSITE *St Paul's, London: technical pen and watercolour,* S/S

Card player, Spain: Edding pen, S/S

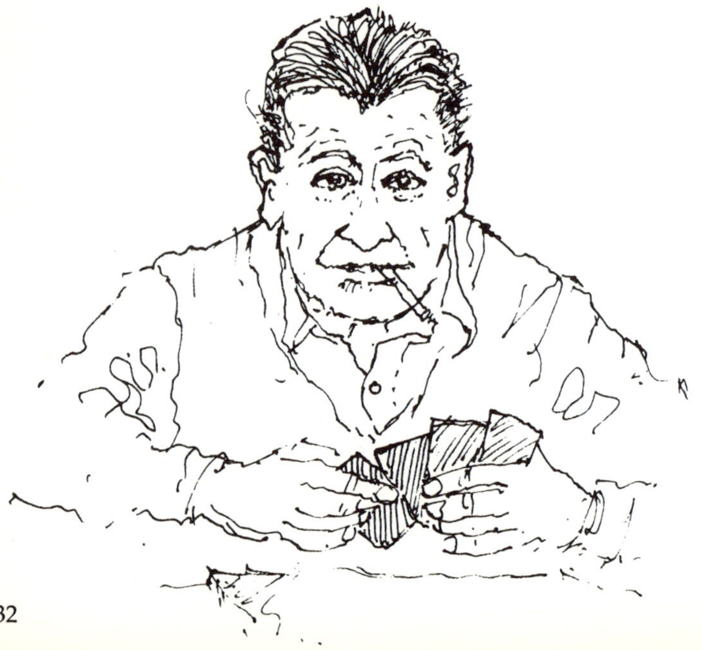

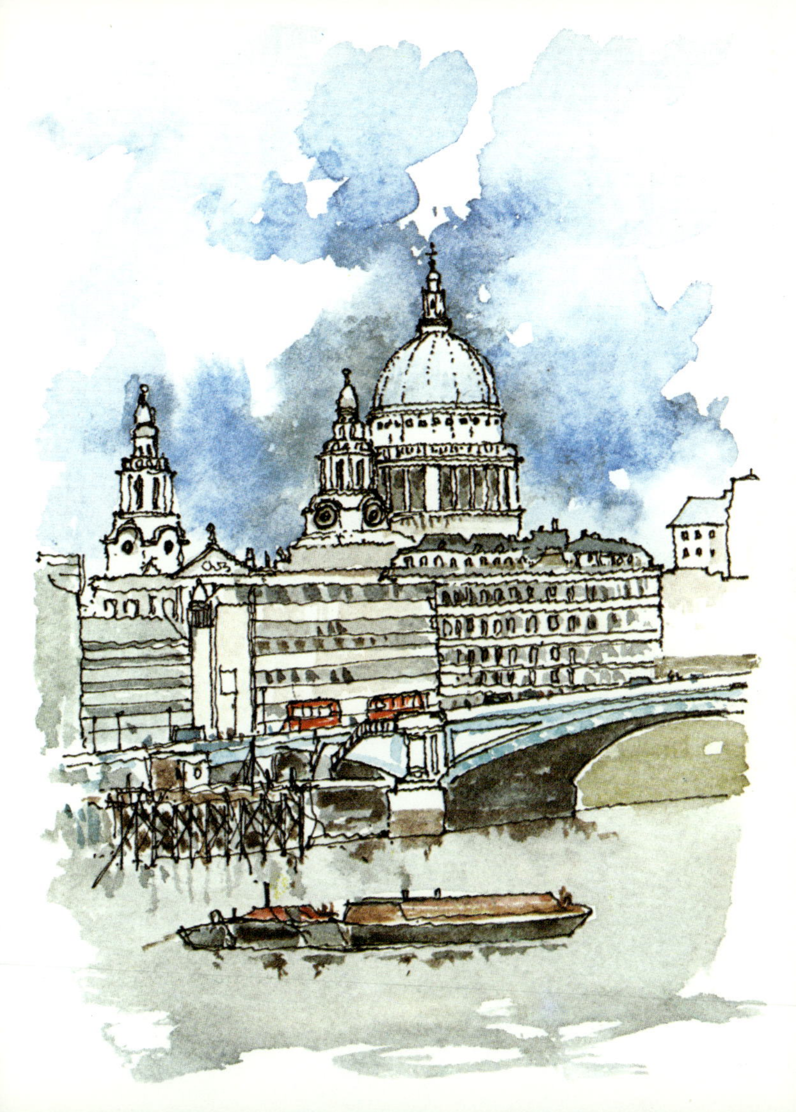

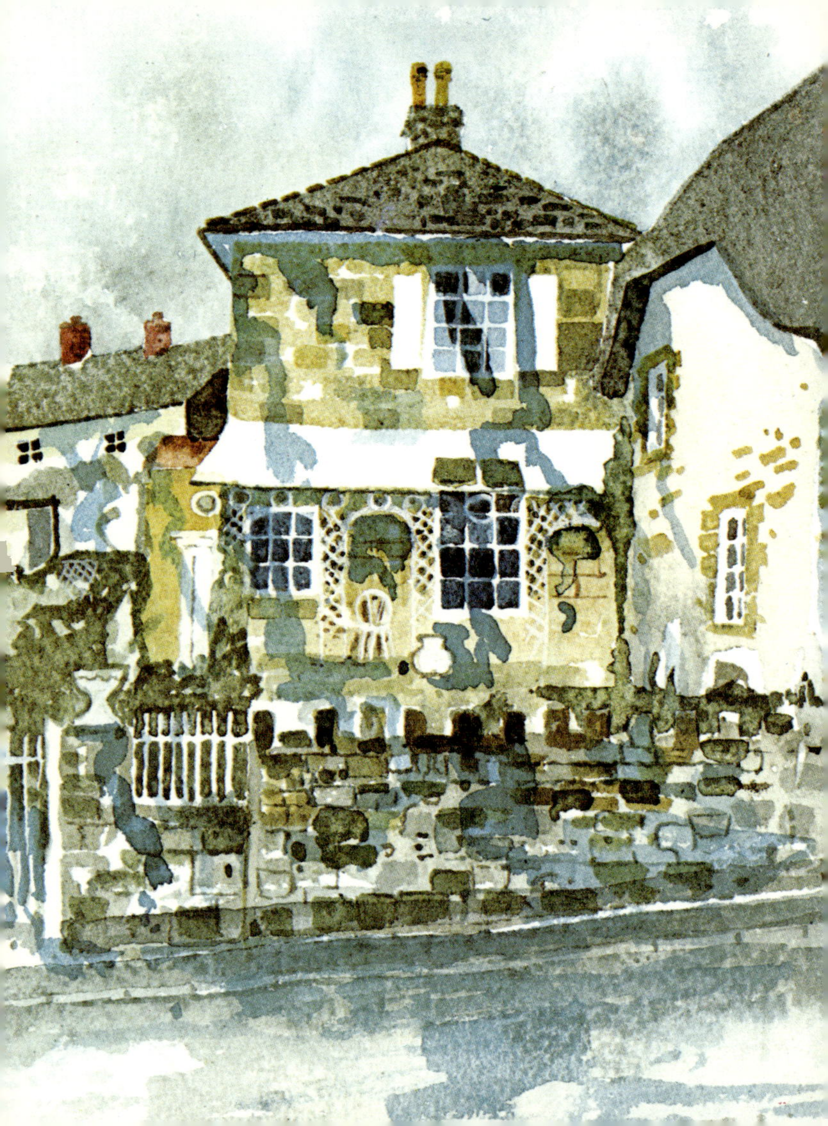

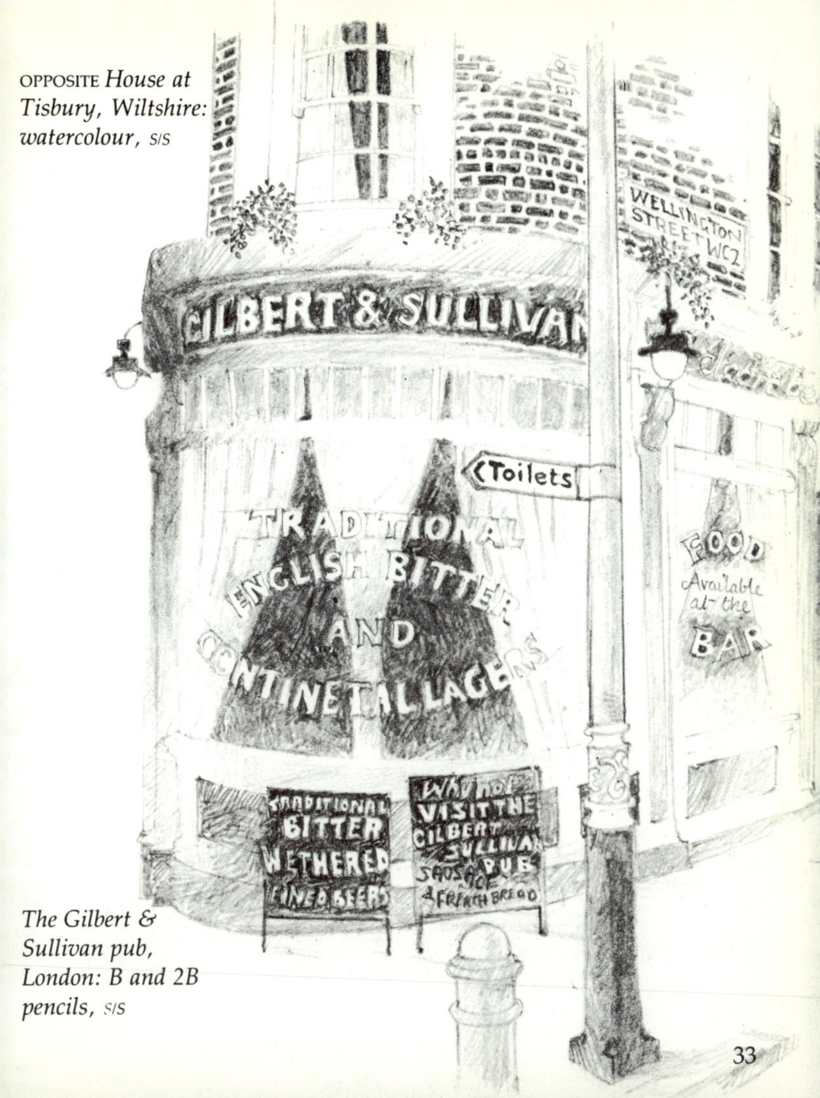

OPPOSITE *House at Tisbury, Wiltshire: watercolour,* S/S

The Gilbert & Sullivan pub, London: B and 2B pencils, S/S

PERSPECTIVE AND SCALE

Perspective is a complex but fascinating subject and there are many good technical books around on the subject. It is not my intention, therefore, in this pocket guide to sketching, to spend too much time on it, but I have tried to illustrate some of the problems with different sketches and drawings.

One simple approach to understanding perspective, is to go outside with a transparent ruler and hold it at eye level, parallel to the horizon. Move the ruler up and down, always keeping it horizontal. You will immediately see which lines go down to the horizon and which go up.

In my drawing opposite you can see how the lines of the walls and telegraph poles converge at the horizon, and how the trees, stones and birds all diminish in size further into the distance.

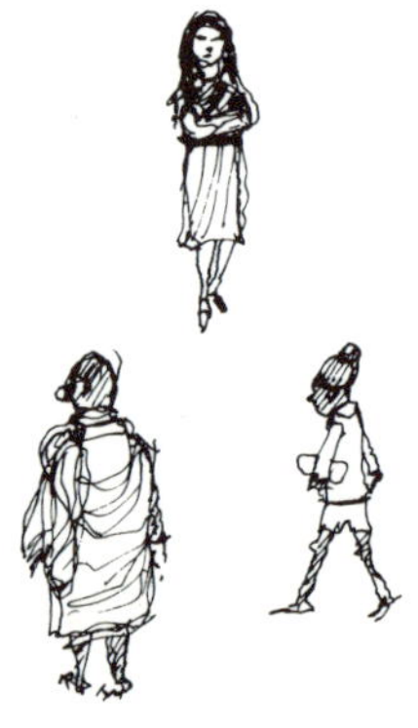

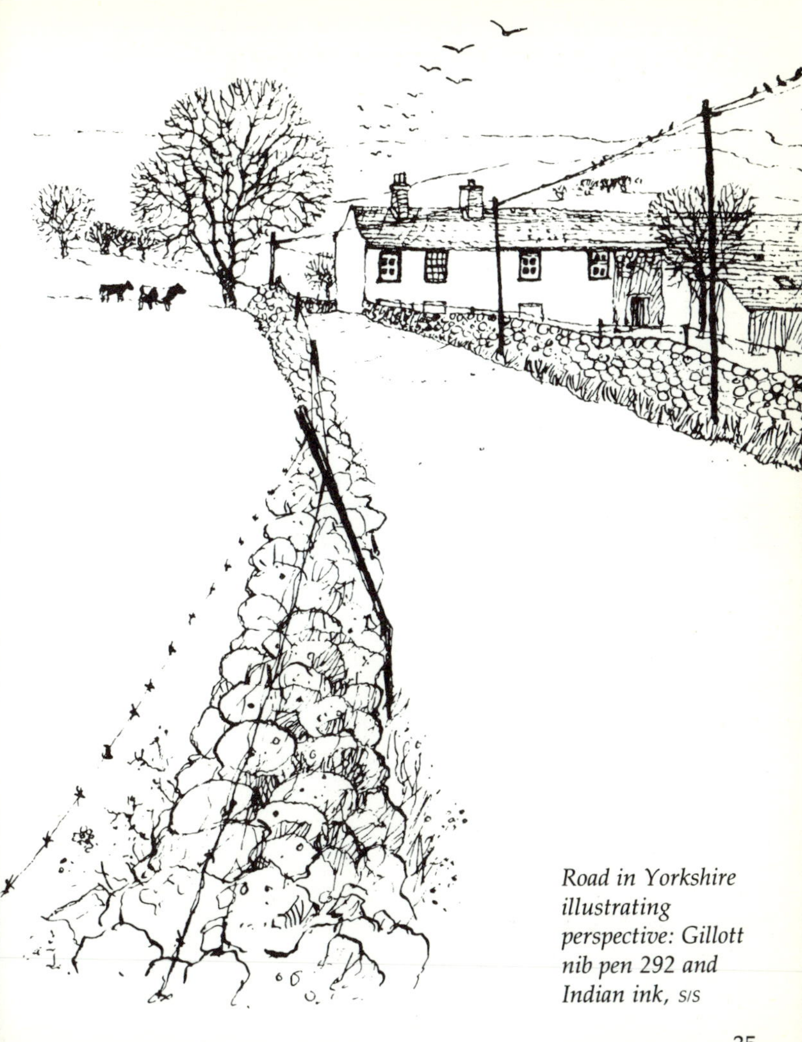

Road in Yorkshire illustrating perspective: Gillott nib pen 292 and Indian ink, S/S

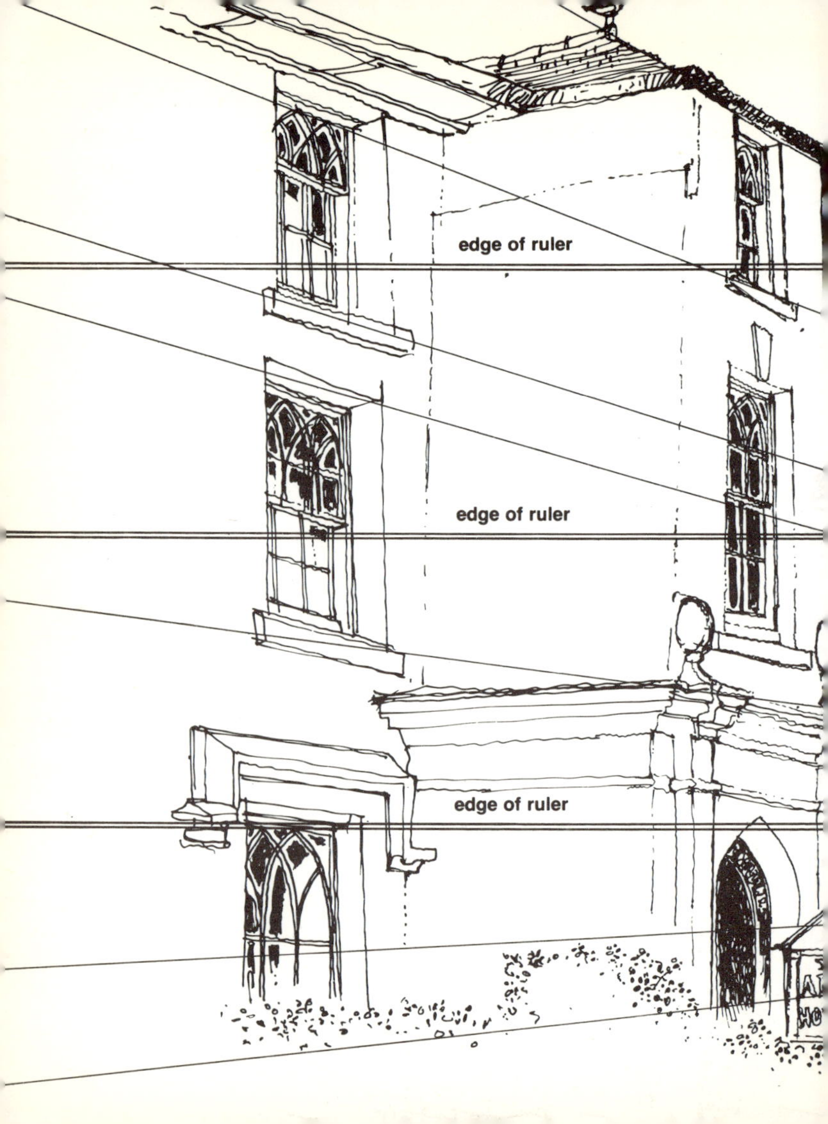
edge of ruler
edge of ruler
edge of ruler

My drawing of the Abbey Hotel in Penzance was drawn on the spot without any conscious thought of perspective but I have overlaid a number of lines to illustrate the 'ruler method'.

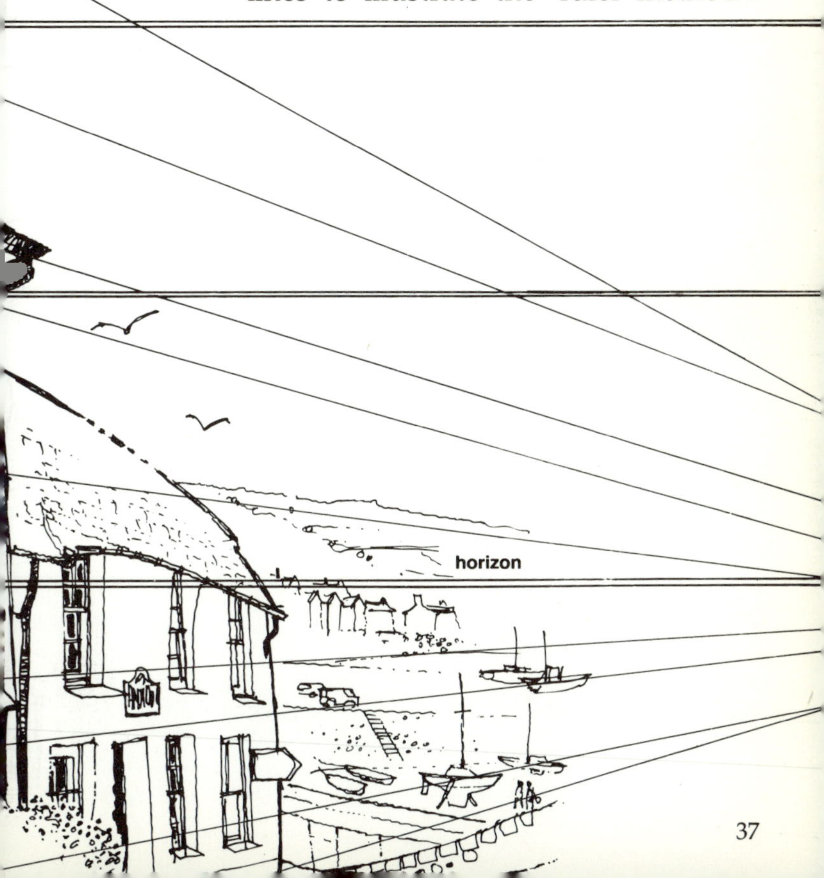

Abbey Hotel, Penzance: fountain pen, 9½ × 7½ in (240 × 190 mm)

When drawing buildings always keep a constant check on these horizontal lines with a ruler or long pencil all the time you are sketching.

It is easier to show perspective in a drawing with buildings but you can also portray it by using different gradations of tones. Tones will get lighter in the distance than in the foreground. And, of course, animals, people, trees, etc., will all recede in size as they get further away.

I used the ruler method again in my sketch of Hebden Bridge. From my vantage point I could see that the roofs of the houses near the top of the town were parallel to the horizon at eye level, even though each house was built on a slope and stepped up one from the other. Lower down you can see that the street on the left is sloping upwards and the houses are again stepped up. However, the houses in the street on the right, which also slopes up towards eye level, are not stepped up. Here the roofs slope upwards in a straight line parallel to the street.

Hebden Bridge, Yorkshire: technical pen, 6½ × 5½ in (165 × 140 mm)

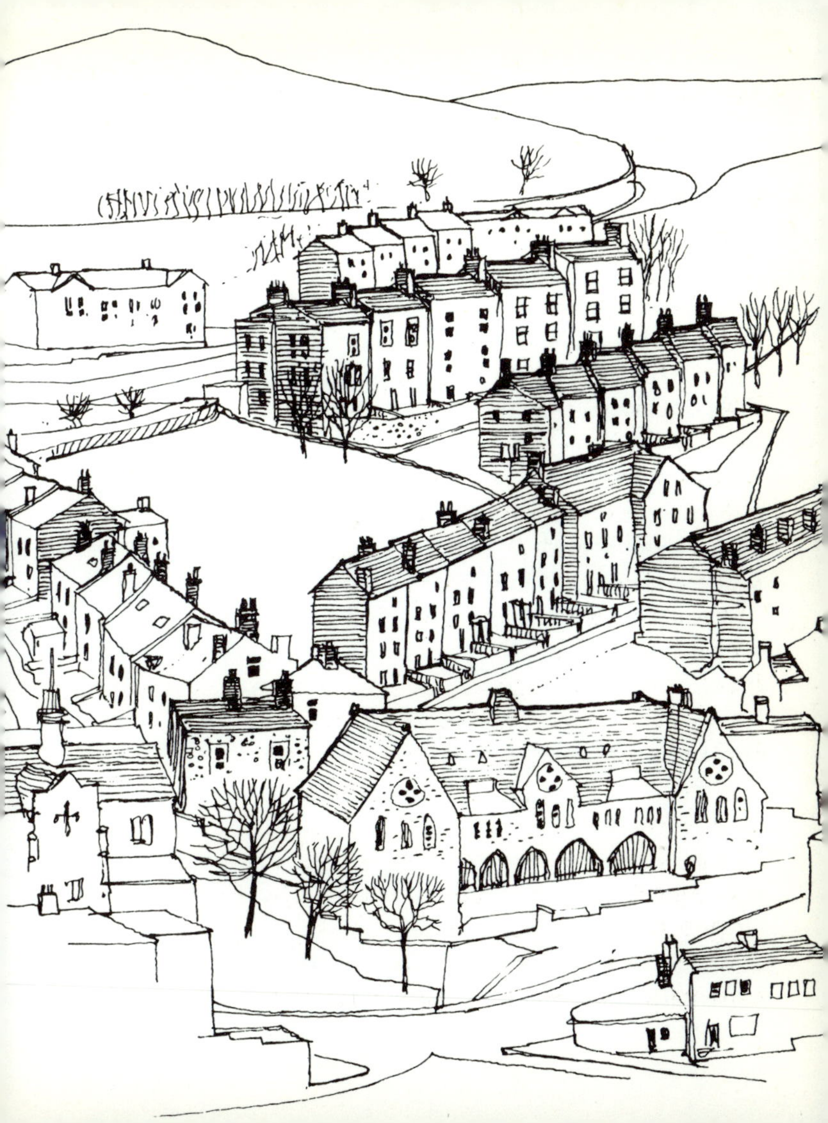

Proportion

Proportion and scale set the scene for a drawing and bring it to life in the same way as the scenery and backcloth on a stage set lend scale to the actors. Proportion is of vital importance if you want your drawing to look realistic. If you are drawing architecture, then the windows and doors must be in the correct proportion to each other, to the building itself, and to any people in the scene.

Andalucían landscape: technical pen, 4½ × 6 in (115 × 152 mm)

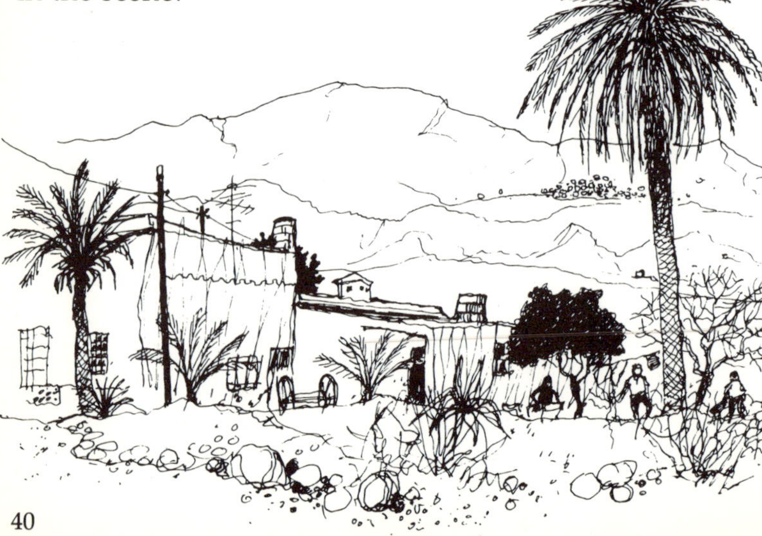

One good way of judging scale is to hold your pencil or pen in a vertical position at arm's length in front of you, shut one eye and measure the height of your subject, be it a figure or a window, by moving your thumb until the height of the subject is the same as the distance between the top of your thumb and the pencil point. By using this measure you can assess how many times the subject will go into the height of the building. Continually check and recheck while you are sketching.

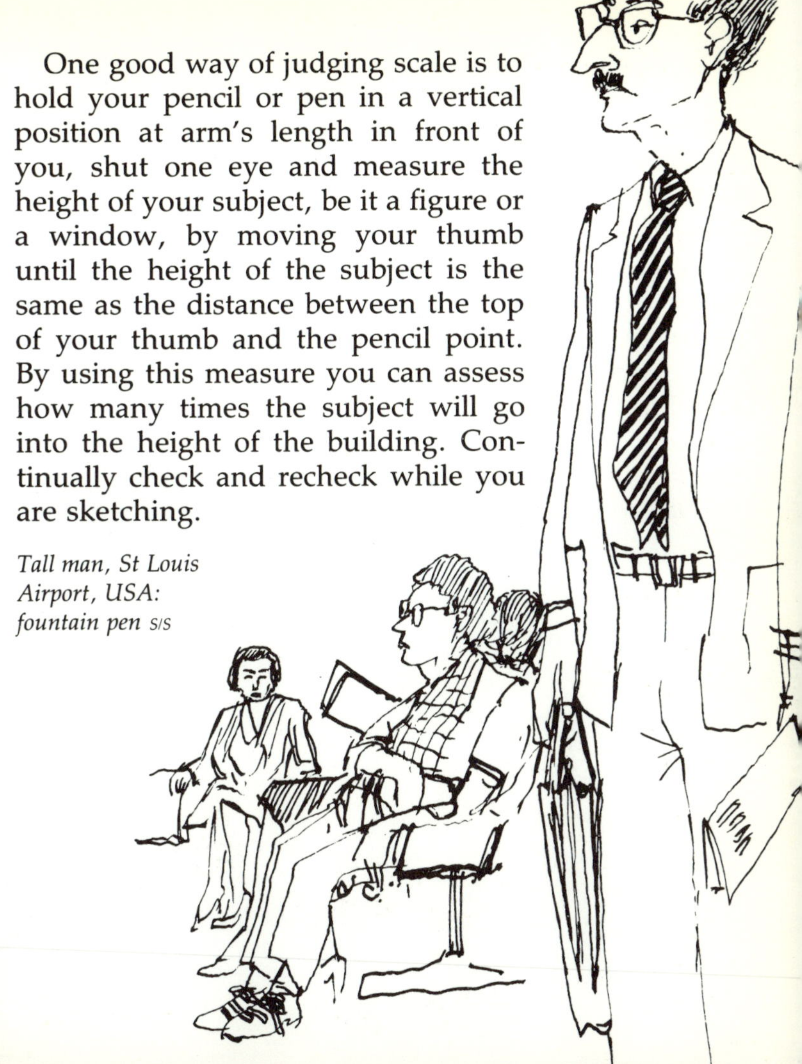

Tall man, St Louis Airport, USA: fountain pen S/S

Look at the drawing of Chicago to see how this would work. I have used the people and cars in the foreground to accentuate the enormous size of the skyscrapers in the background. In the sketch of Ironbridge, although a very quick sketch, I have shown the scale of the bridge by relating it to the size of the buildings seen through the arch.

Ironbridge, Shropshire: fountain pen, 5 × 3½ in (128 × 90 mm)

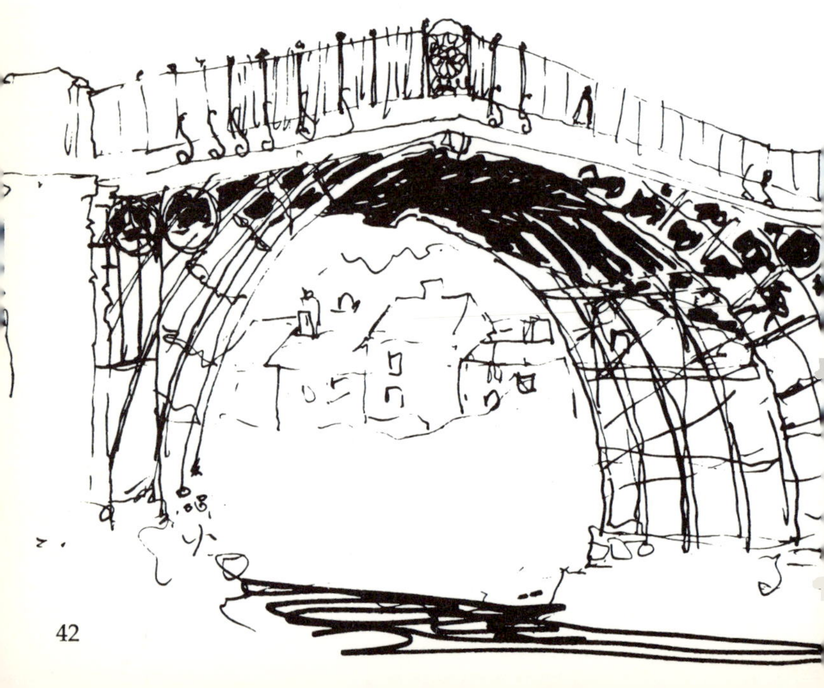

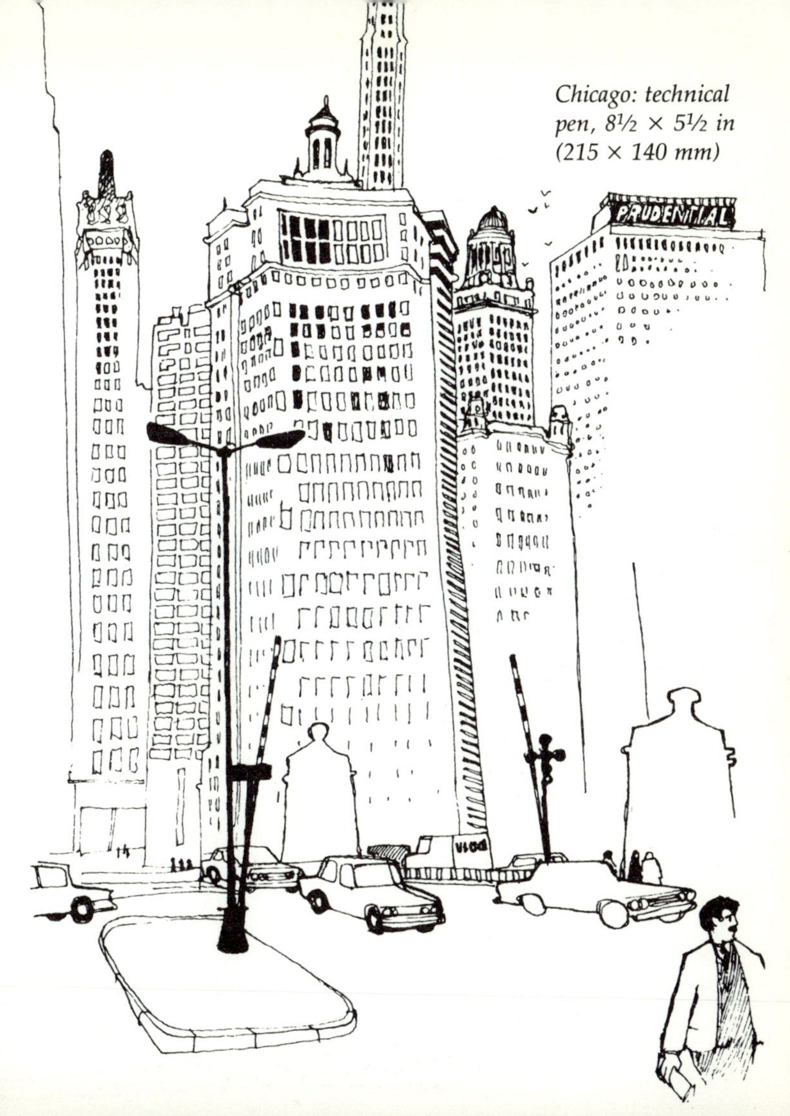

Chicago: technical pen, 8½ × 5½ in (215 × 140 mm)

TONAL VALUES

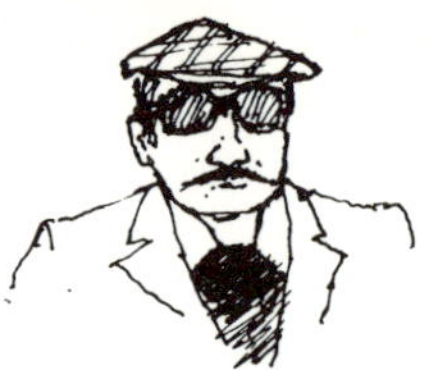

KGB, MI5 or CIA? technical pen, S/S

Tonal values in a drawing can be likened to musical notes. The Italian word *chiaroscuro* (which means the use of contrast in a picture) itself has a musical sound. The primary use of tone in a sketch is to make the darkest tones appear close to the eye and the paler tones recede into the distance. If you look at a landscape in the mist of the early morning or evening this will be obvious to you. Generally the darkest tones and the lightest lights are in the foreground, and the tones gradually merge into each other in the distance. By holding the chart opposite against a scene it will help you to see how the tones recede.

Dark areas in a sketch can be used to emphasize the area itself or to accentuate by contrast a light area next to it. However, sometimes the tones do not always recede in the distance, for

OPPOSITE *Tone chart: Gillott nib pen 303 and gouache, 8½ × 6½ in (215 × 165 mm)*

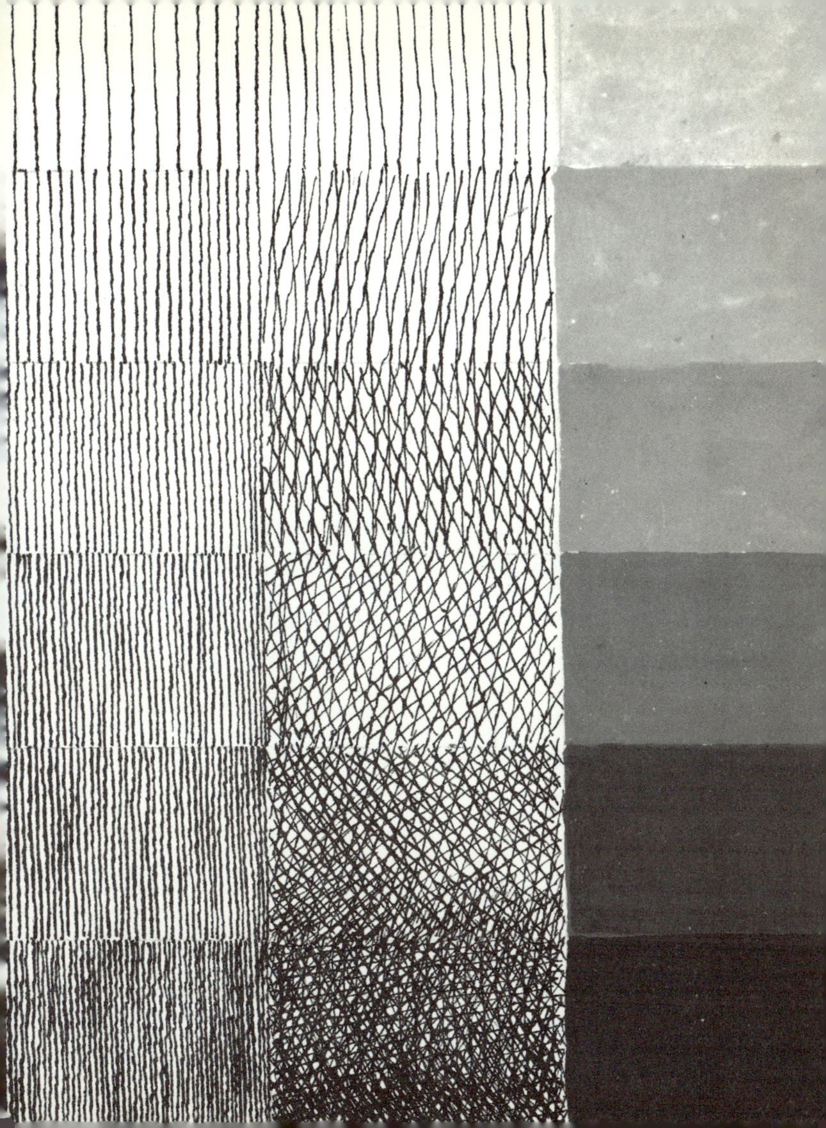

if a dark shadow is cast by a cloud, say, in the middle distance of your picture, this can make distant hills darker than those in brilliant sunshine in the foreground. A white cottage can be made to look more brilliant by dark thunder clouds behind it. Dark areas of a drawing should not only be used to emphasize the receding landscape beyond, but also to make patterns and to balance the whole composition.

Alston: pen and wash, 5 × 4 in (128 × 100 mm)

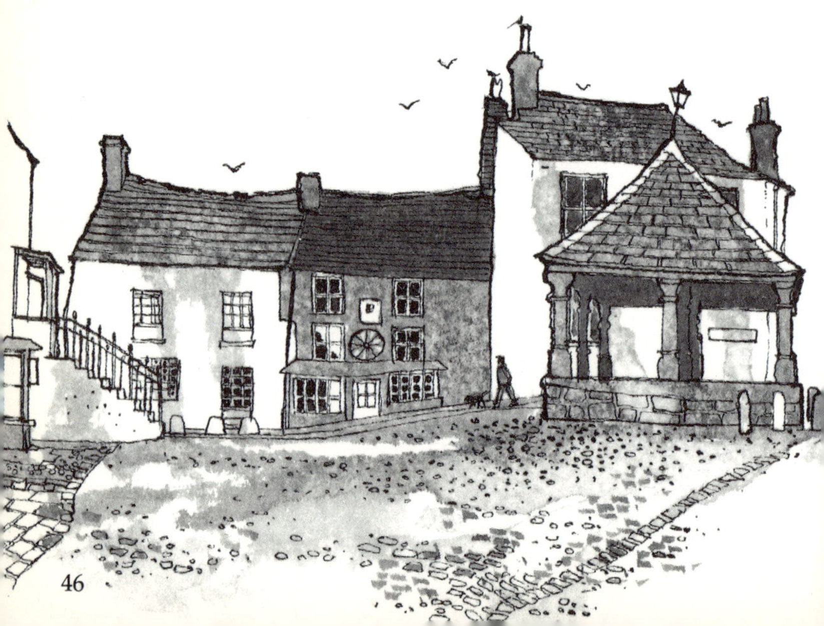

I have selected drawings in this section which show how to use different tones to make patterns and shapes, as well as to demonstrate distance. For example, the pen drawing of Mojácar overleaf illustrates how cross-hatching can be used to convey the correct tonal values of a receding landscape, and also at the same time, the atmosphere of the gathering gloom of a Spanish winter's evening.

Chaise longue: Rotring 0.18, S/S

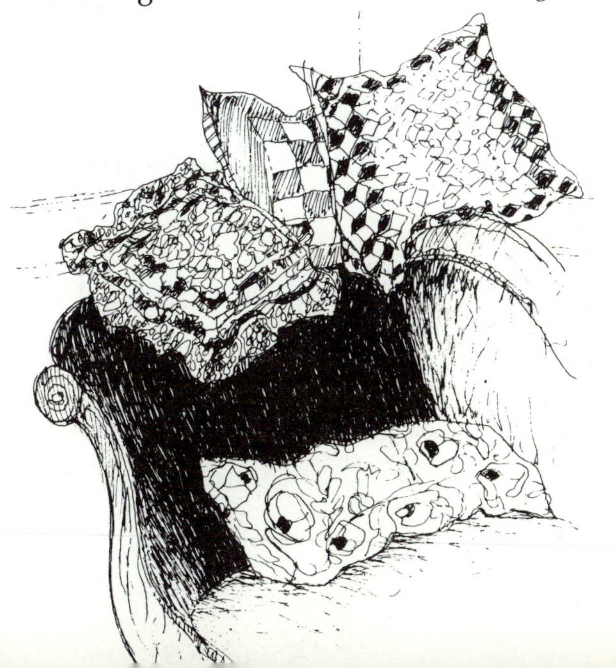

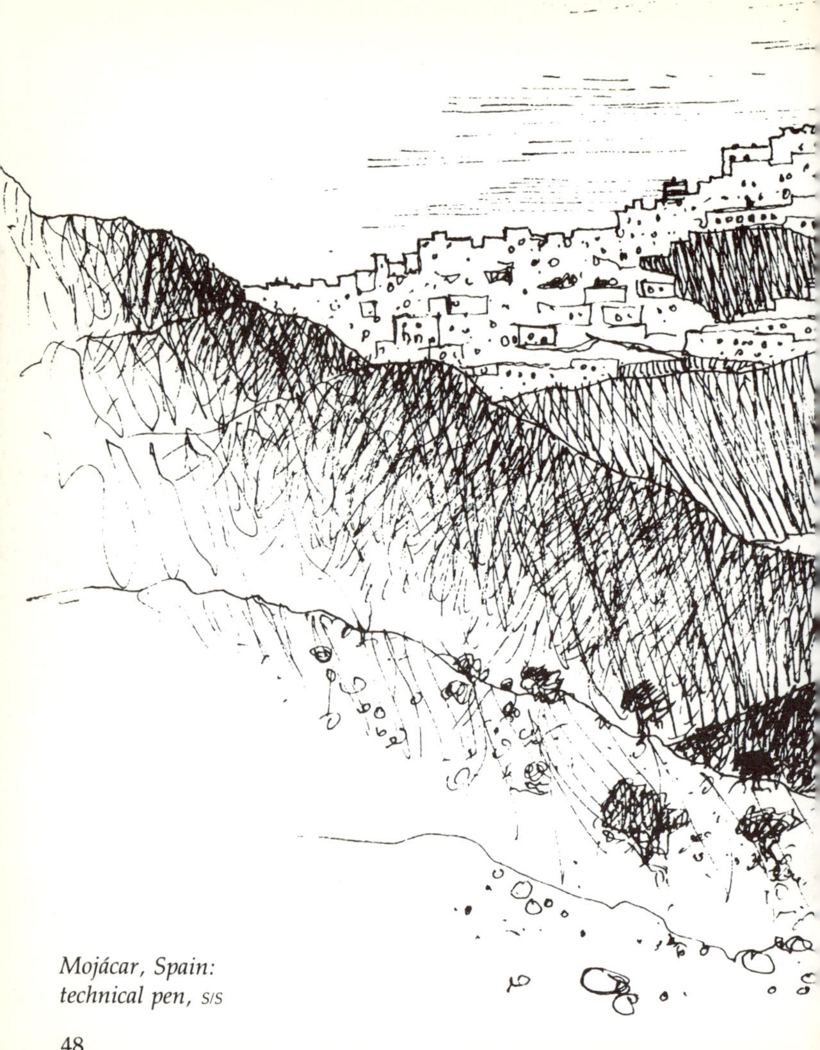

Mojácar, Spain:
technical pen, S/S

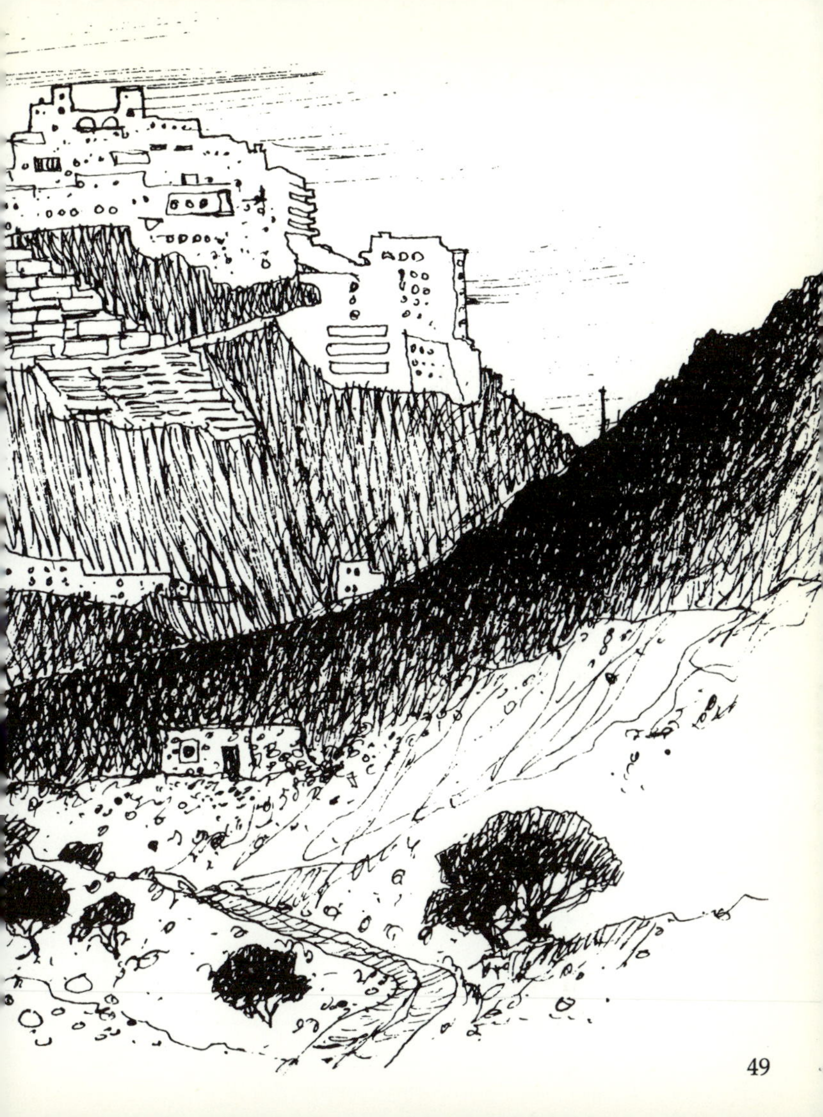

COMPOSITION

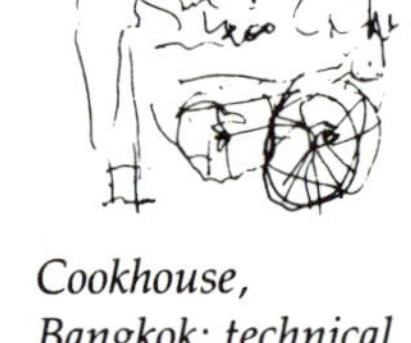

Cookhouse, Bangkok: technical pen, S/S

In my opinion this is the most important section of the book. The art and skill of picture making is of paramount importance to both artists and photographers and it has to be learned by experience. If the composition of a picture is weak then all the other technical skills cannot rescue that picture.

The art of making or composing a picture is an entirely fresh experience with every painting or drawing you do. Each time you are confronted with your subject and the only practical limitation you have is the boundary of the page in your sketchbook. The problem is to decide how much of what you see you are going to use, and to choose a focal point.

The composition of the drawing opposite was interesting because, as it was a cold day, I drew the view from a café window, and I was fortunate to

OPPOSITE *Ludlow, Shropshire: technical pen and wash, 6½ × 5 in (165 × 128 mm)*

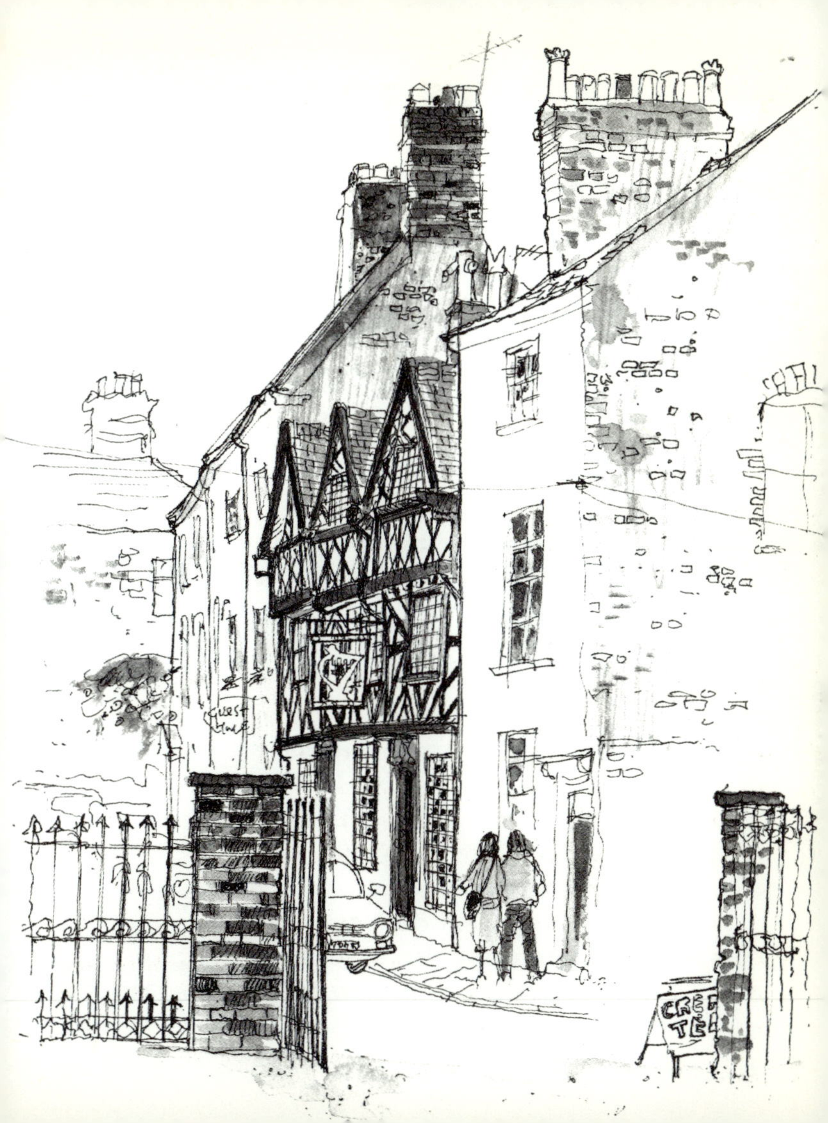

have the gates in the foreground to frame the houses and accentuate distance. Whereas the sketch overleaf of the boat at Lympstone made a good composition for a vertical page.

In this drawing of the coastline near Mojácar in Spain the shape was governed by my viewpoint. There was no foreground of any interest so I left

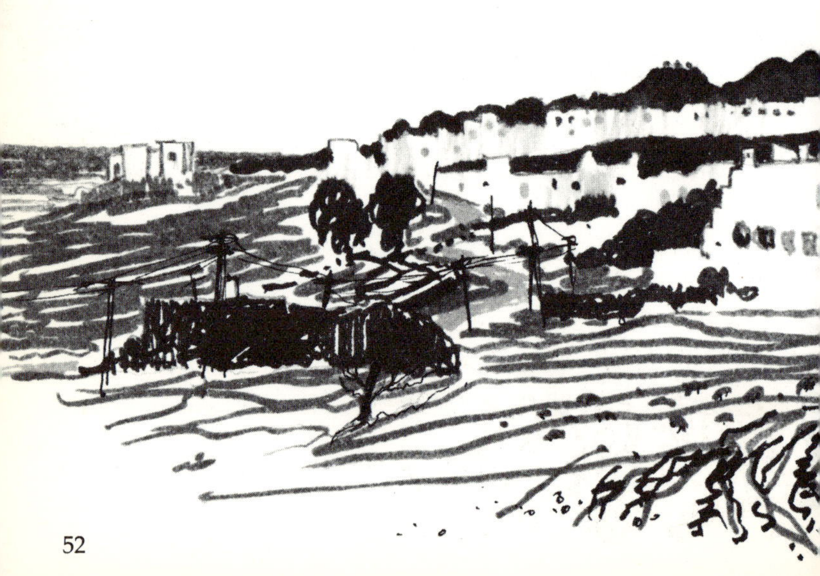

the foreground blank and concentrated on adding tone to the drawing to make the middle and the far distance interesting, thus making the buildings in the middle distance stand out white against a darker background. This is something I talked about in the previous chapter on tonal values.

Almeriá, Spain: coloured felt pens and technical pen, S/S

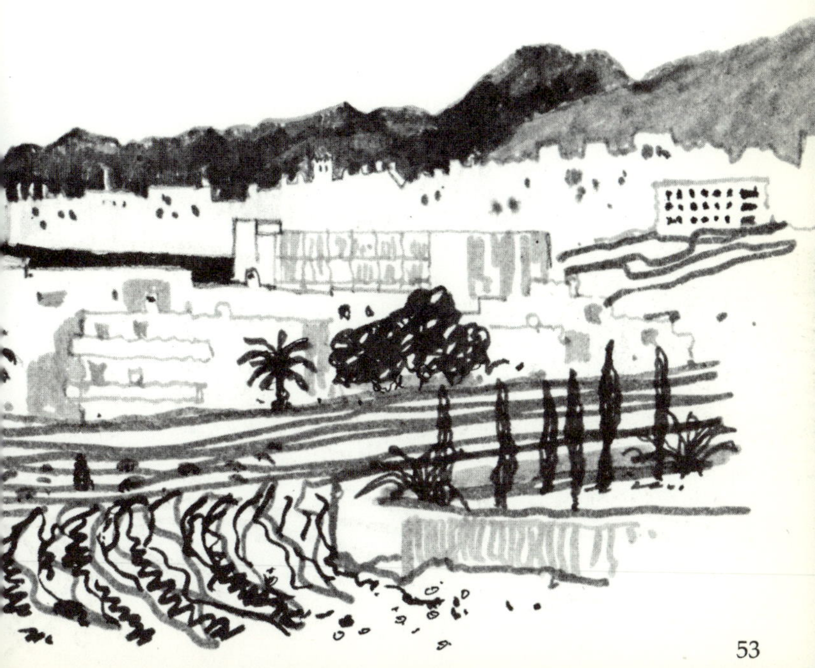

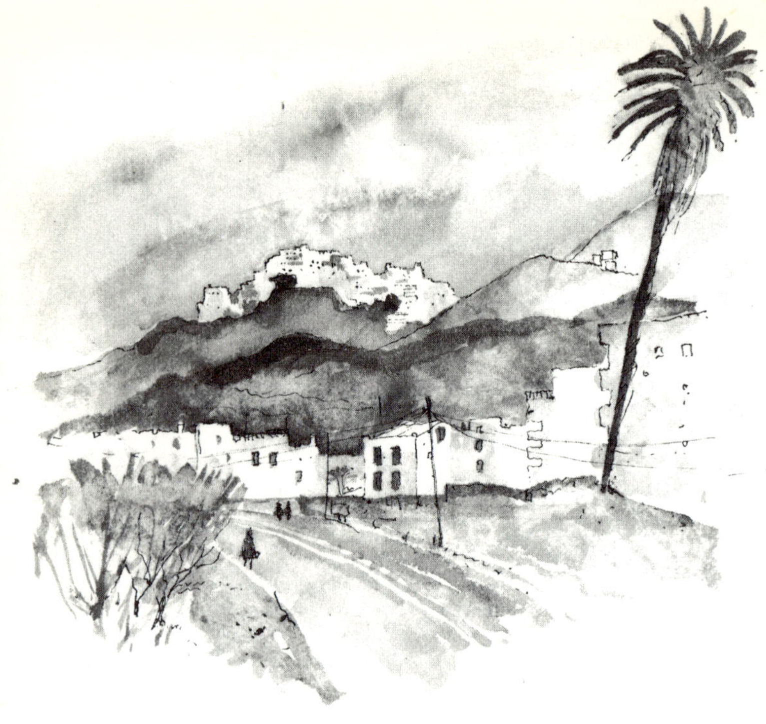

Mojácar from Turre, Andalucía: watercolour and technical pen, 6 × 6½ in (152 × 165 mm)

With a camera, of course, we look through the view-finder and move the camera until we have set the scene that we want to take. In art too we need a view-finder. To make one I suggest you take a piece of card that will fit into the sketchbook you are using and cut an oblong shape like a

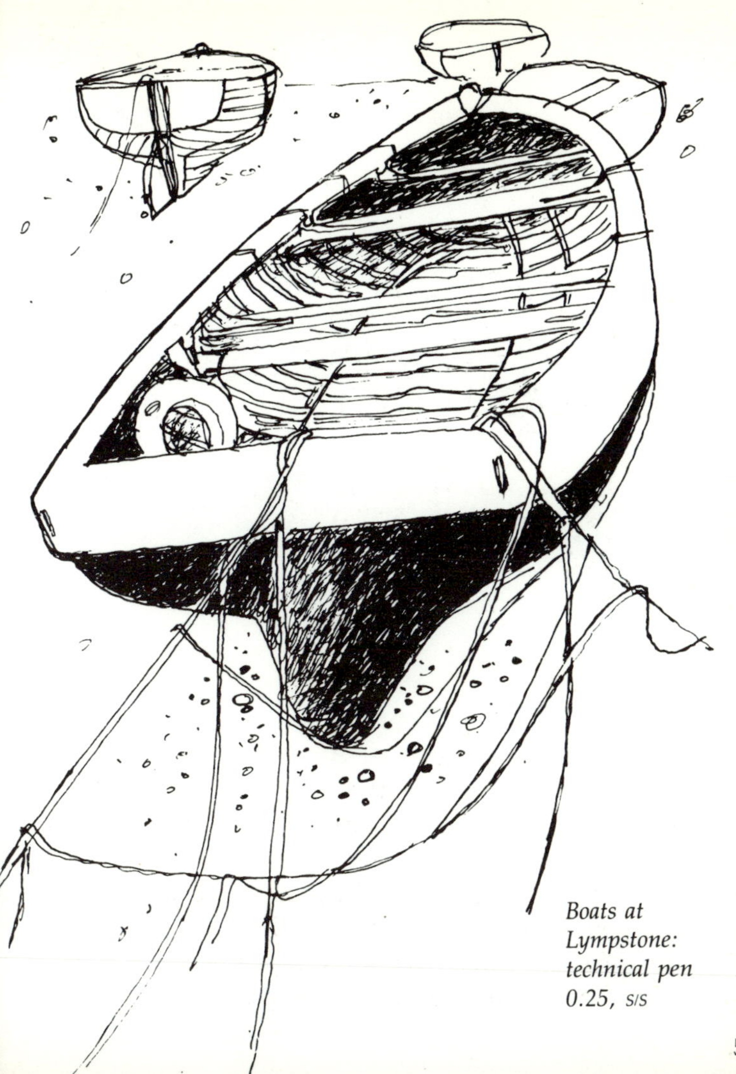

Boats at Lympstone: technical pen 0.25, s/s

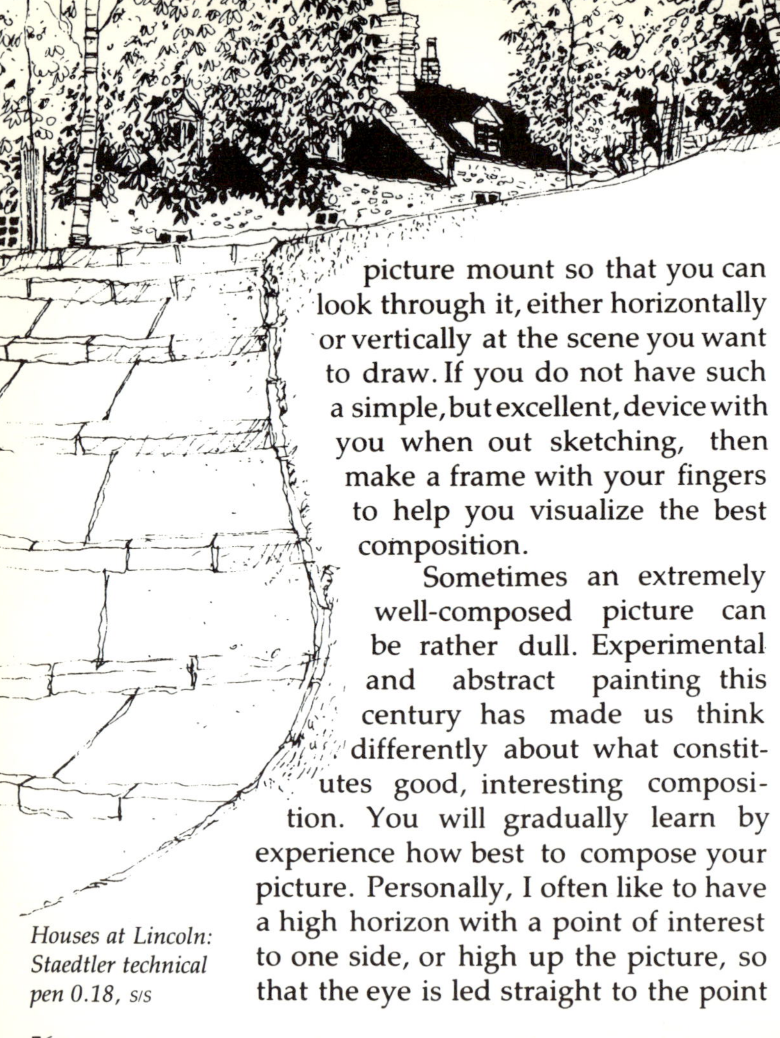

picture mount so that you can look through it, either horizontally or vertically at the scene you want to draw. If you do not have such a simple, but excellent, device with you when out sketching, then make a frame with your fingers to help you visualize the best composition.

Sometimes an extremely well-composed picture can be rather dull. Experimental and abstract painting this century has made us think differently about what constitutes good, interesting composition. You will gradually learn by experience how best to compose your picture. Personally, I often like to have a high horizon with a point of interest to one side, or high up the picture, so that the eye is led straight to the point

Houses at Lincoln: Staedtler technical pen 0.18, s/s

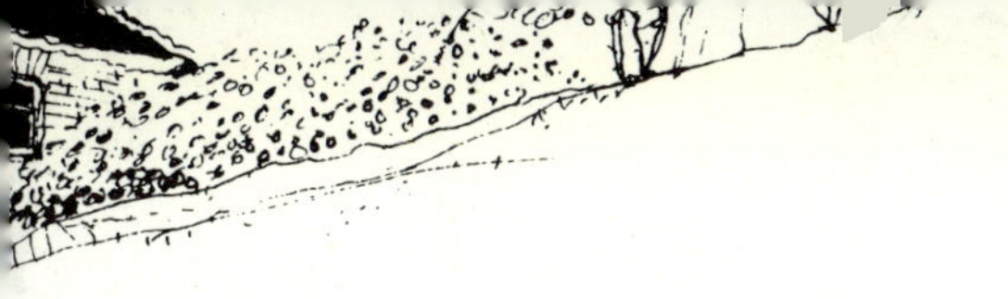

OVERLEAF *Bédar, Spain: dip pen and watercolour on 140lb Bockingford paper, 9 × 6 in (230 × 152 mm)*

of main interest. Obey the basic rules of composition but try to make the drawing exciting and interesting, and remember, you don't have to put everything you see in the picture!

One cottage, white against a mountain, or a stormy sky, or perhaps a single egg on a newspaper strategically placed on a pretty tablecloth – these can be just as interesting compositions as a drawing of a busy street. Try to ensure that the picture has impact and something to say. It is often helpful to study other artists' work, either in your local art gallery or museum, or in art books and to try to analyse why you like them or dislike

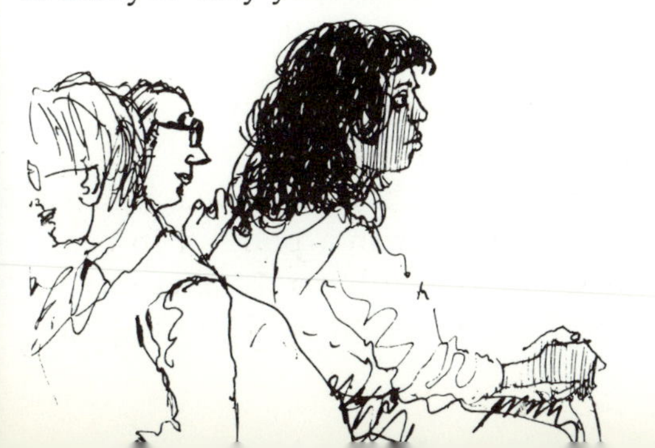

'Waiters': felt pen, 3 × 3½ in (77 × 90 mm)

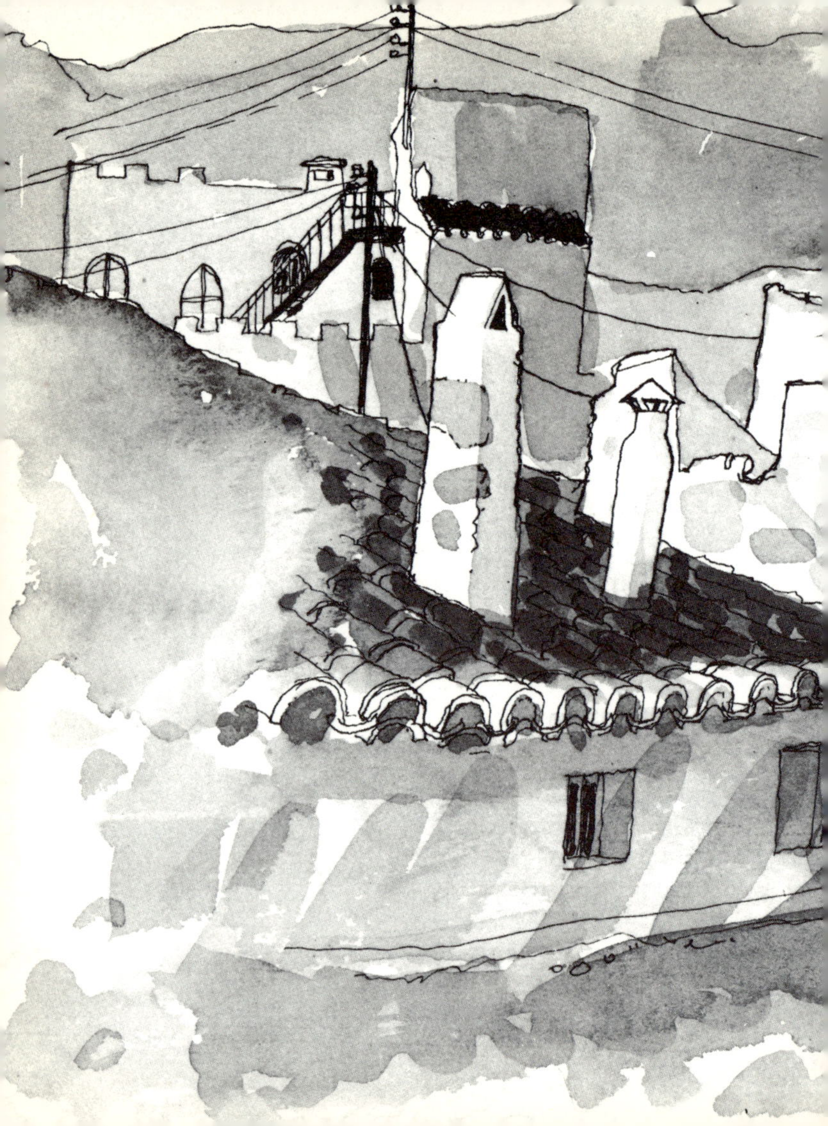

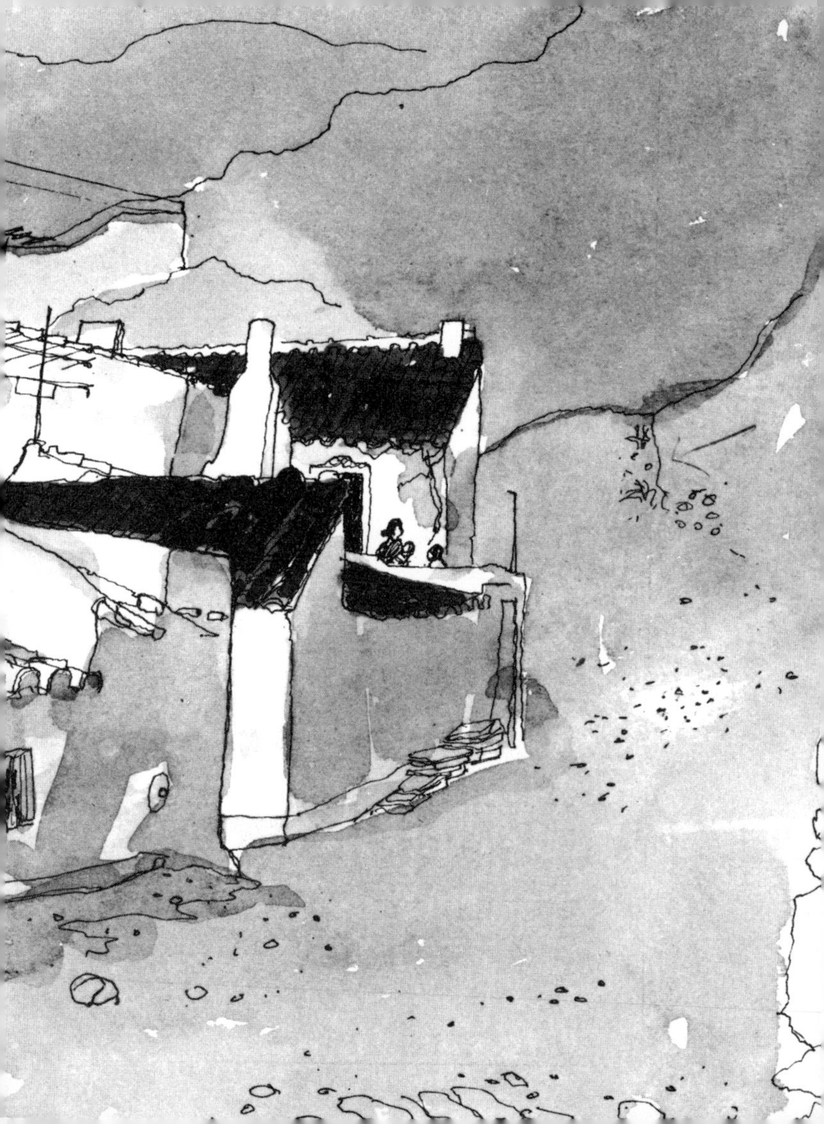

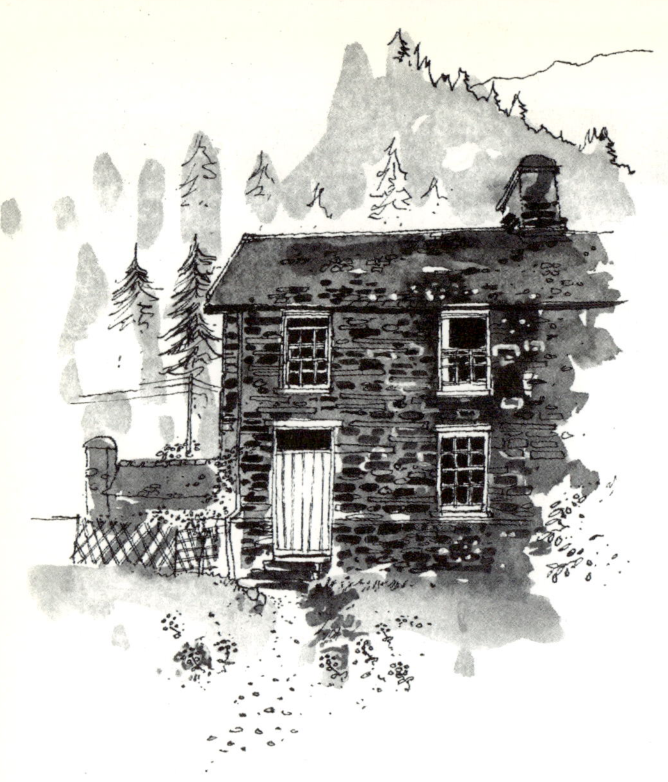

them, in terms of composition, colour, tone and their 'statement'.

Look at the drawings I have chosen to illustrate this chapter and you will notice that I have taken care to design each drawing to fit the shape of the page i.e. its frame. Don't hesitate on

Ancestral home: pen and wash, 5 × 4 in (128 × 100 mm)

OPPOSITE *Wine-dark sea, Greek Islands: pen and ink,* S/S

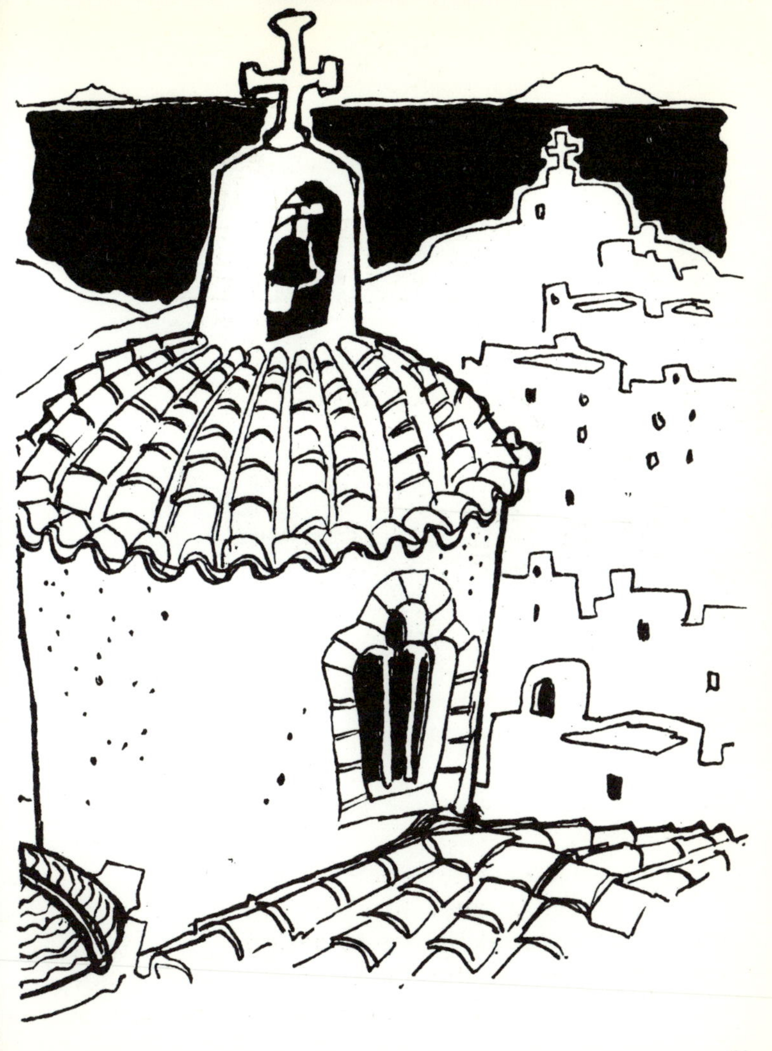

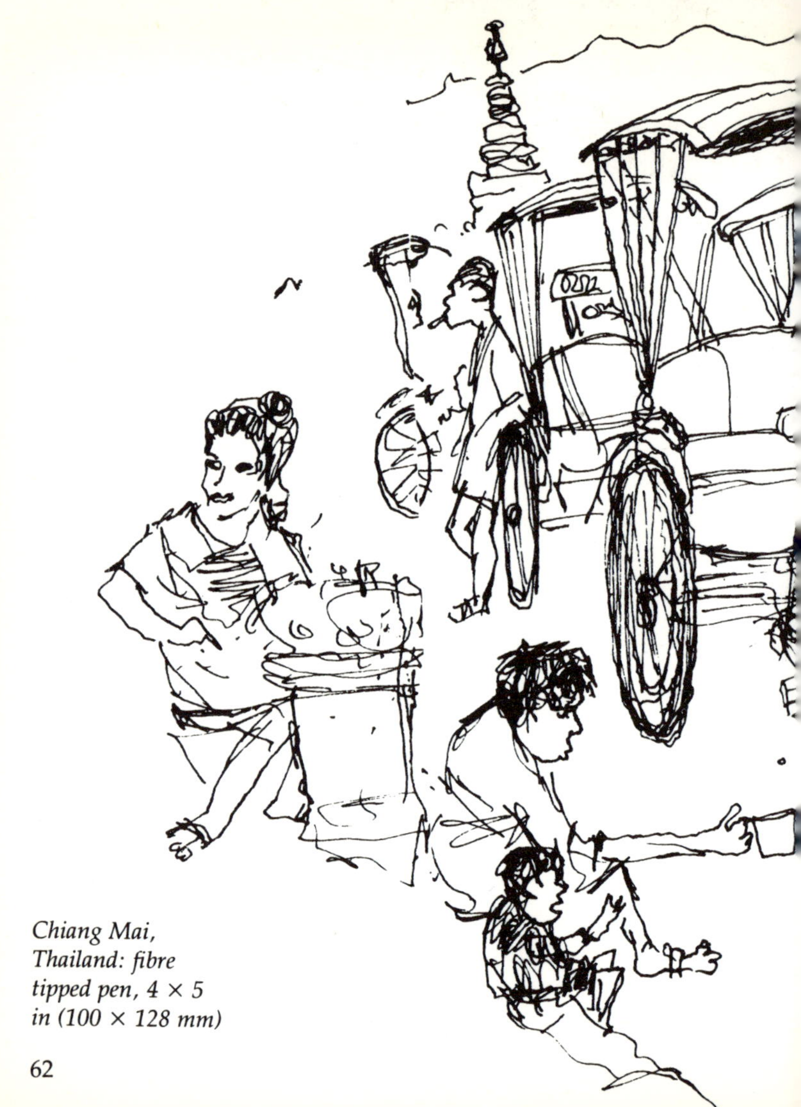

Chiang Mai, Thailand: fibre tipped pen, 4 × 5 in (100 × 128 mm)

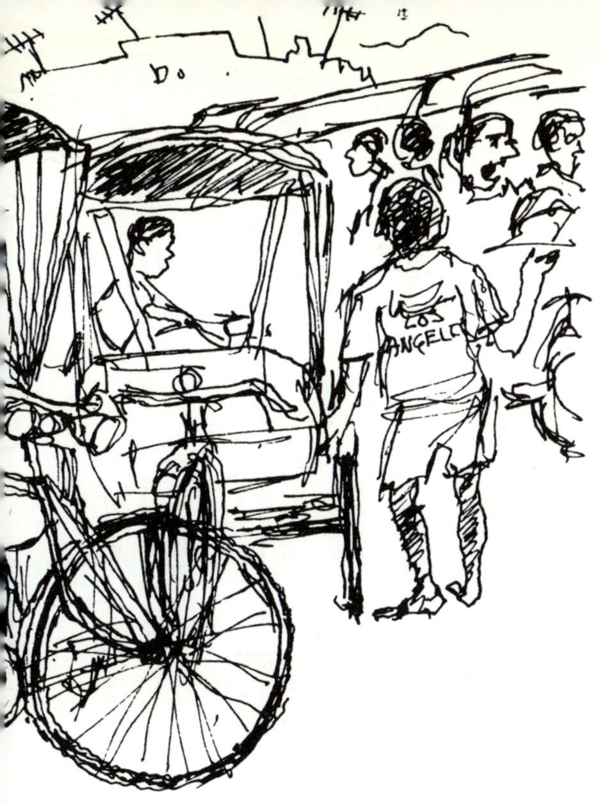

occasion to draw across both pages of a sketchbook.

When I was drawing this street scene in Chiang Mai, Thailand I thought that I would get the drawing on one page of my sketchbook, but I soon realized that it would have to go

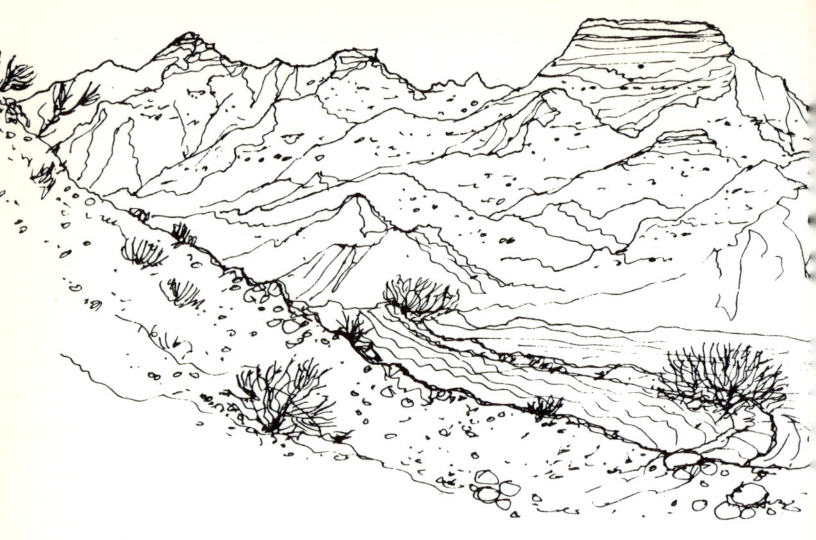

across two pages. However, this can look quite effective from time to time.

You can, of course, use your 'viewfinder' in reverse, when, on returning home, a finished sketch or drawing looks hopeless. Cut a mount out of card (I keep a selection of different sized ones in my studio), place it over the sketch and move it about. You will be surprised at how interesting a section of a piece of work can appear, which you thought was a failure.

Andalucían landscape: technical pen, 3½ × 6 in (90 × 152 mm)

OPPOSITE *Winter trees, Dorset: Rotring 2000 Isograph pen, 6 × 4½ in (152 × 115 mm)*

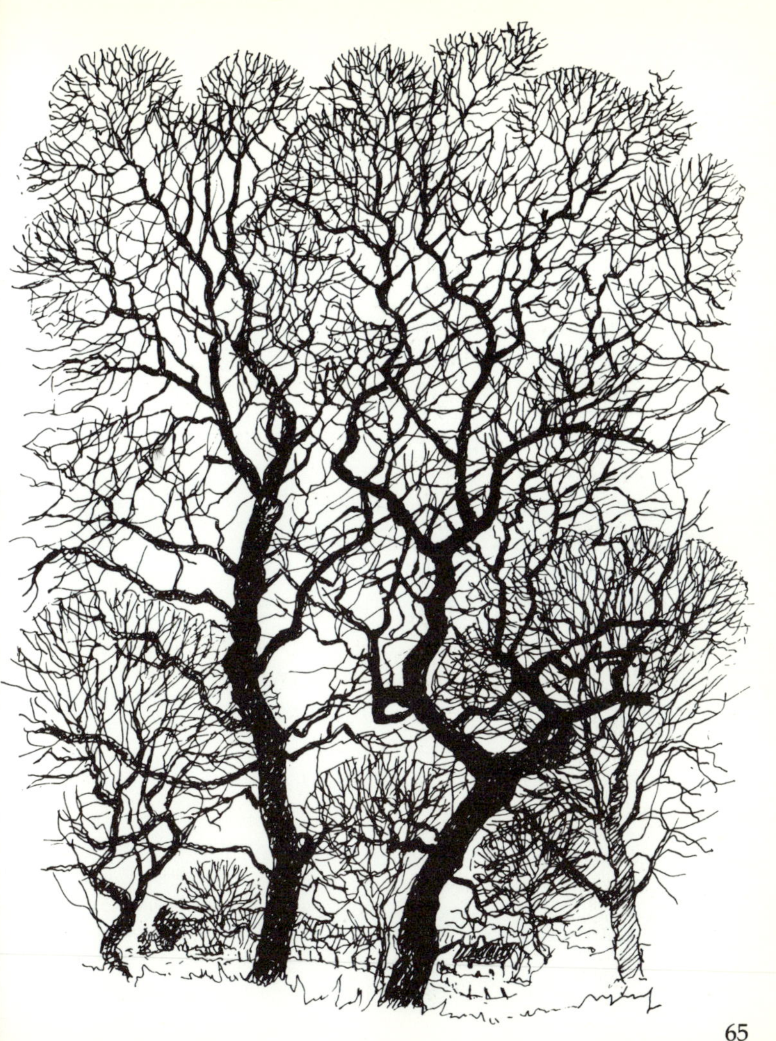

ATMOSPHERIC EFFECTS

This chapter could be entitled 'making the most of the elements'. Turner often made pencil sketches with notes on the spot and then used them to dramatic effect in pictures and sketches. He had a good memory, and a lively imagination, and he reasoned that the elements often changed the subject too fast to record accurately on the spot, except by quick fleeting sketches, with colour introduced at a later stage, back home in the studio. It is fascinating what can be done from simple sketches in the field expanded with imagination later, when perhaps working under more ideal conditions.

Try to use the elements to your advantage in your drawings. The extraordinary landscape of Yellowstone Park overleaf, made me feel very humble and dissatisfied with my efforts to catch such transient beauty.

Stream at Llanfihangel-y-Pennant: pen and wash, 8 × 5 in (200 × 128 mm)

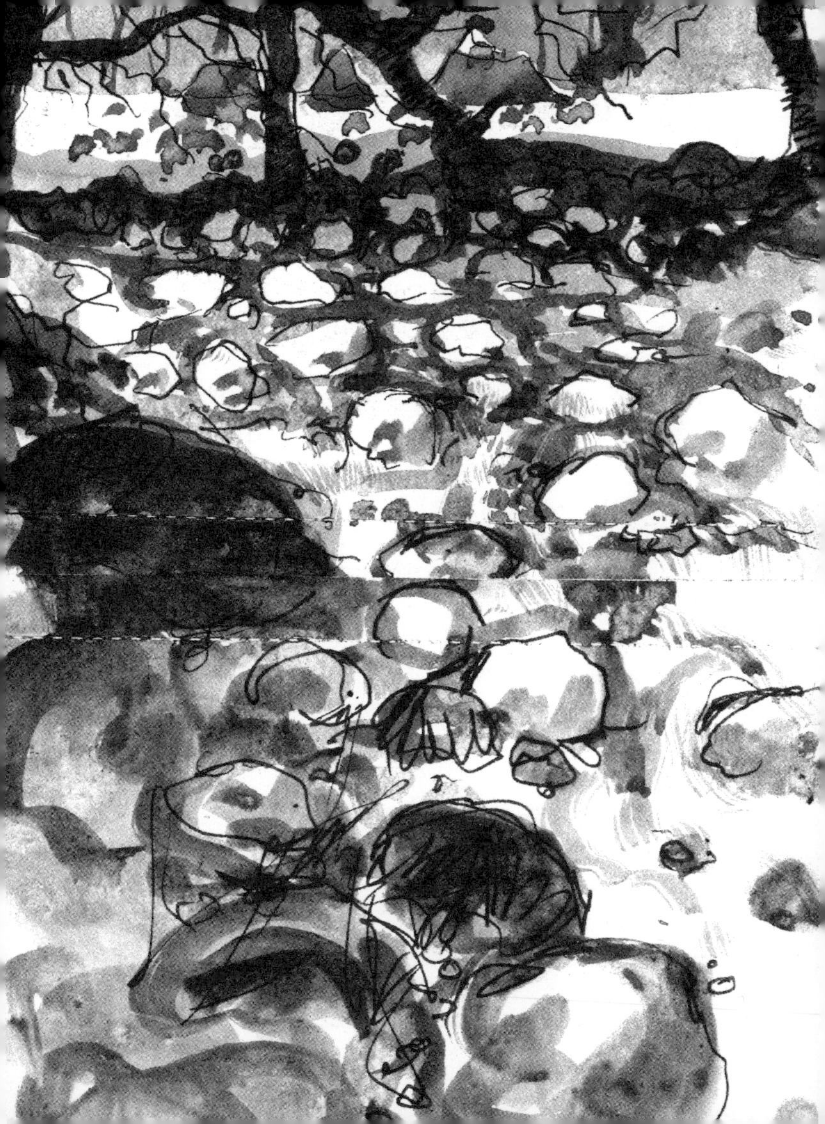

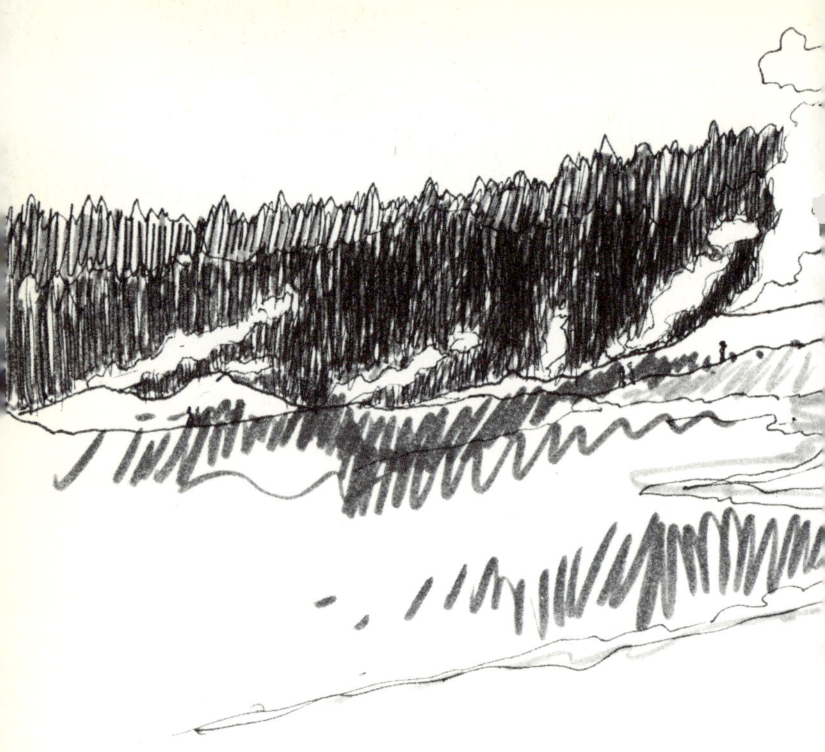

I caught the sparkling light and dark shadows of the stony stream on page 67 by using pen and wash, and I was able to capture the brooding atmosphere of an approaching storm in my drawing of the Welsh farmhouse overleaf with pen and watercolour.

Old Faithful Geyser, Yellowstone Park, USA: coloured felt pens, S/S

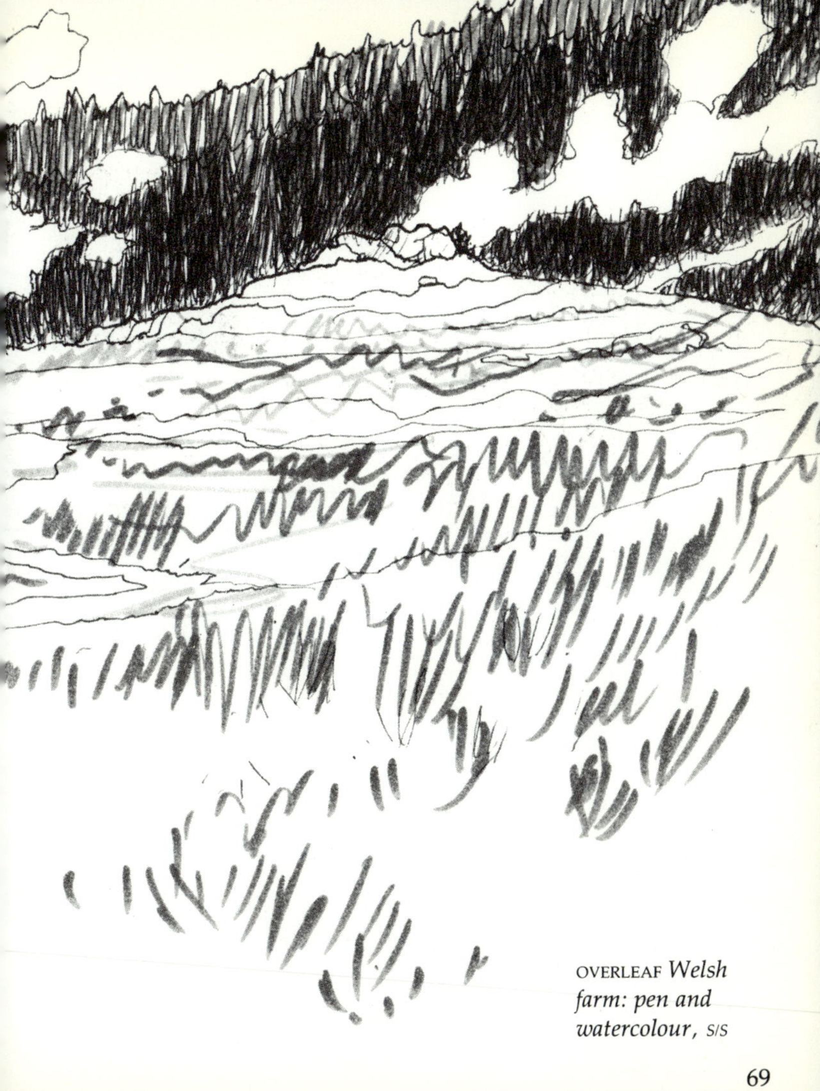

OVERLEAF *Welsh farm: pen and watercolour*, S/S

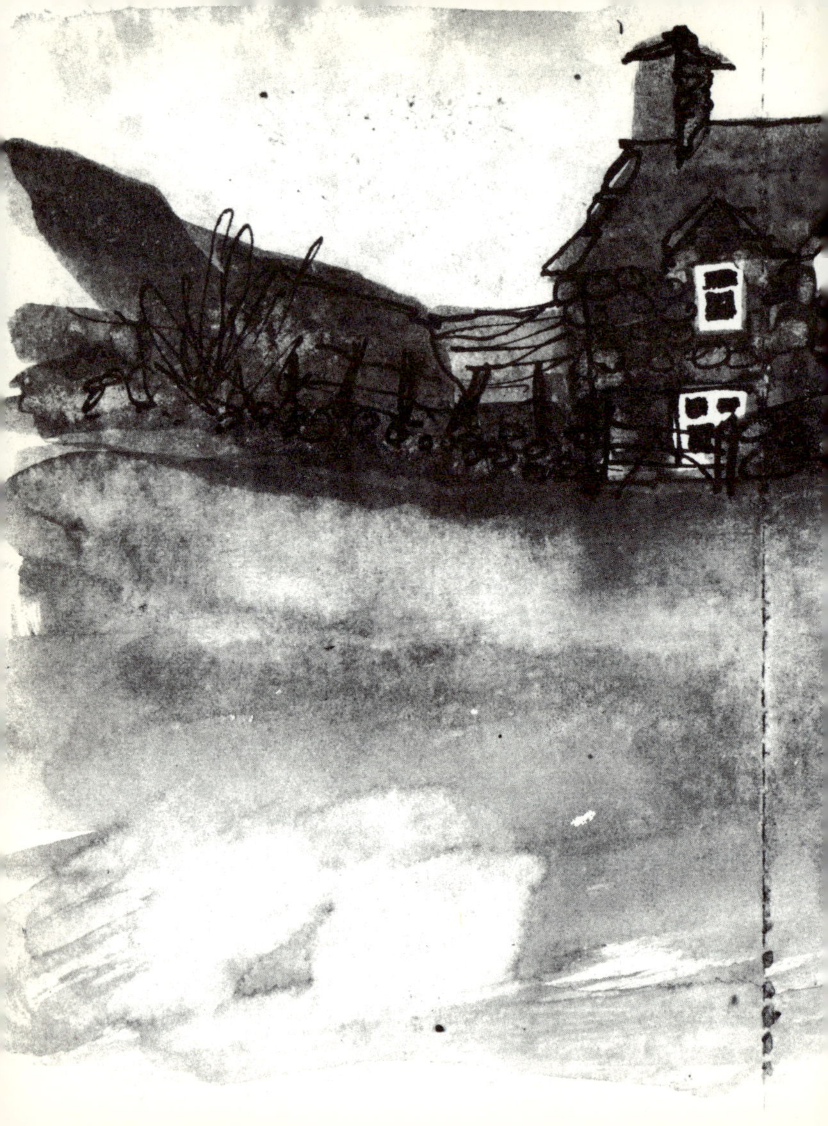

PEOPLE AND ANIMALS

Whether on a tube train in London, or watching drivers wash their elephants in Thailand, I am constantly drawing when I am travelling. Most of the time I use a small sketchbook the size of this book – a new one is dated and titled for each major trip and I try to fill it during the weeks that follow.

OPPOSITE *Baby elephant, Thailand: fountain pen, 2½ × 1¾ in (65 × 45 mm)*

RIGHT *Snooker player: fountain pen, 3½ × 4 in (90 × 100 mm)*

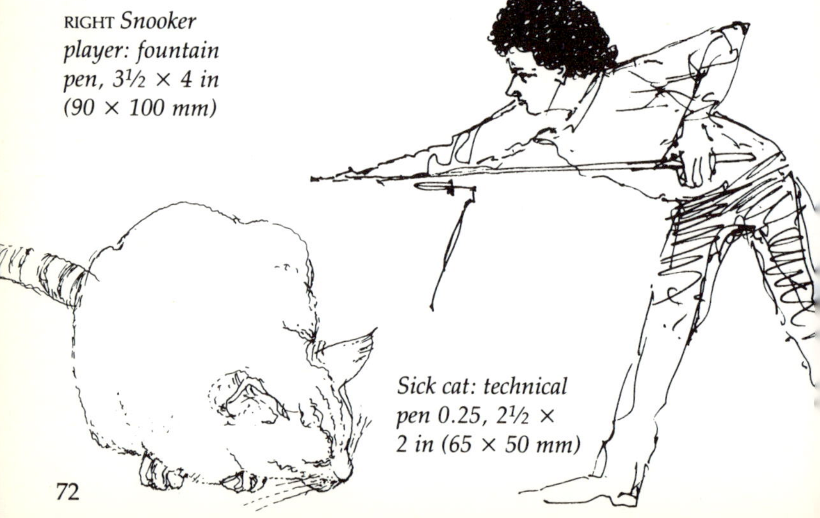

Sick cat: technical pen 0.25, 2½ × 2 in (65 × 50 mm)

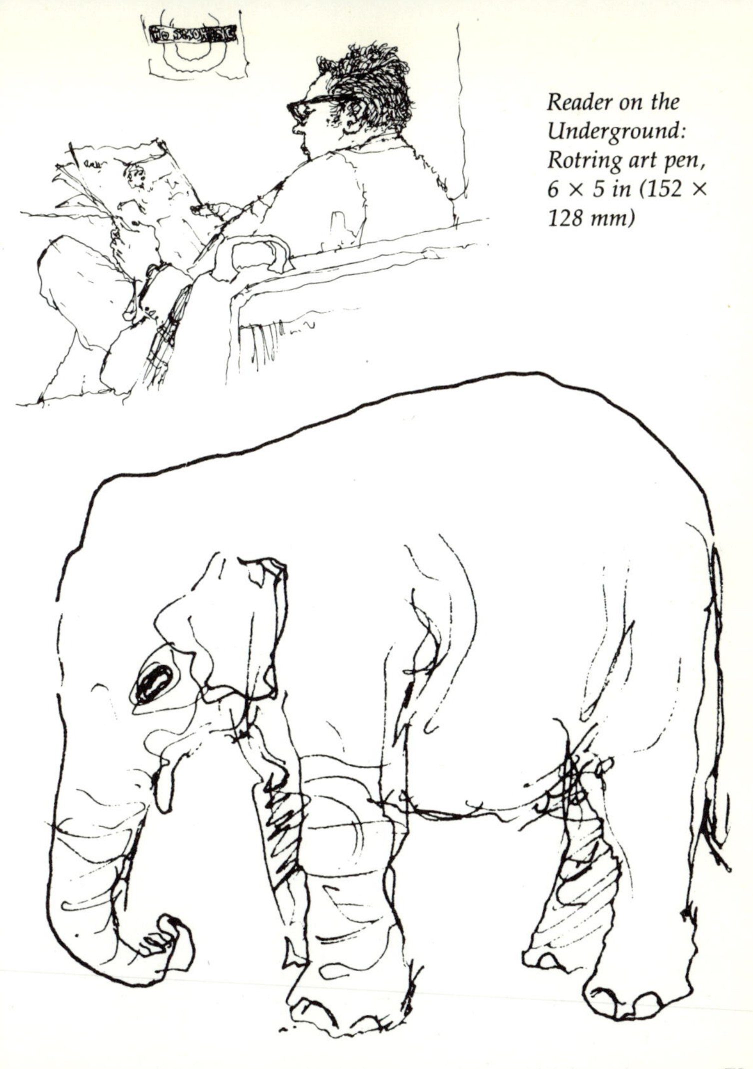

Reader on the Underground: Rotring art pen, 6 × 5 in (152 × 128 mm)

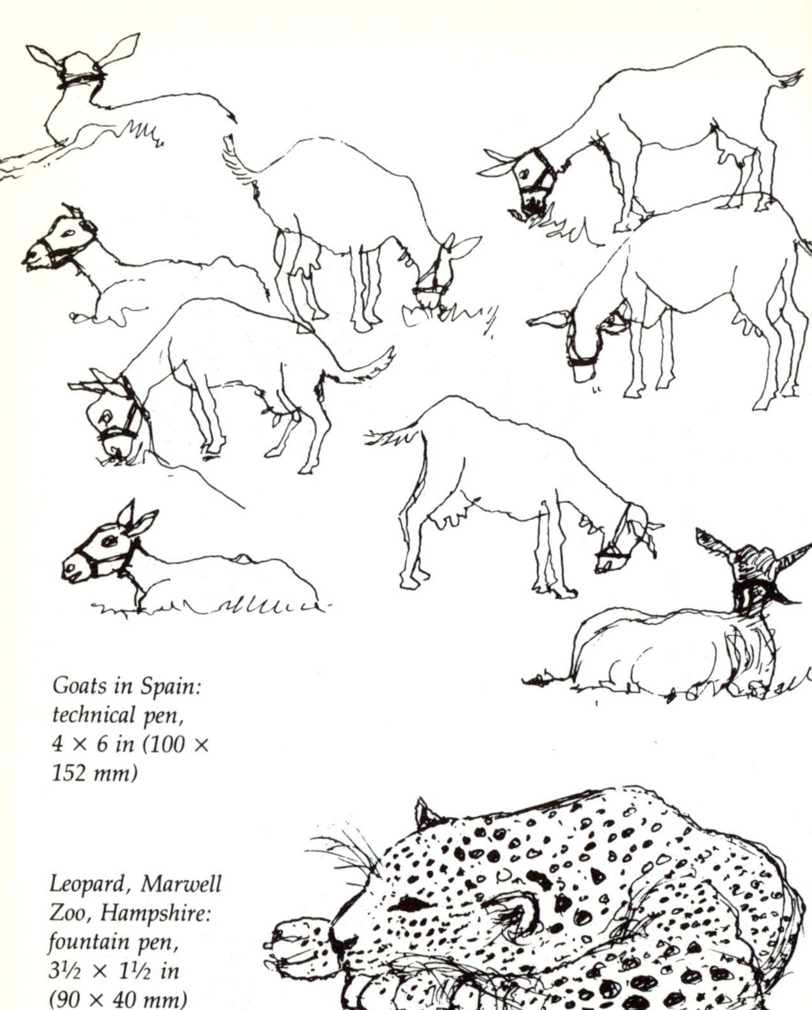

Goats in Spain: technical pen, 4 × 6 in (100 × 152 mm)

Leopard, Marwell Zoo, Hampshire: fountain pen, $3\frac{1}{2} \times 1\frac{1}{2}$ in (90 × 40 mm)

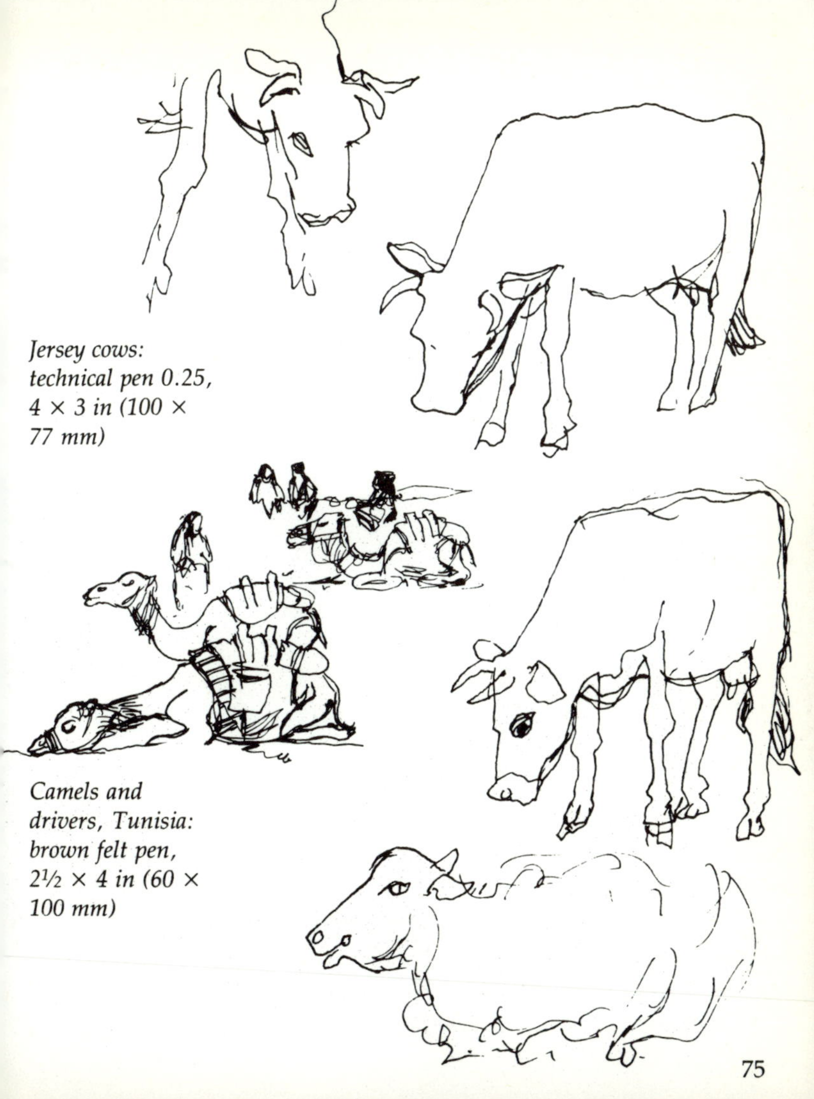

Jersey cows: technical pen 0.25, 4 × 3 in (100 × 77 mm)

Camels and drivers, Tunisia: brown felt pen, 2½ × 4 in (60 × 100 mm)

People are a constant part of our daily life; even when walking the desolate and barren hills of Southern Spain in winter it was not long before I met a solitary shepherd with his herd of goats. Even when walking alone in those hills I am always on the look-out for movement, perhaps of a hoopoe or some other bird, for we inhabit a world full of movement and life. And it is the word 'movement' that frightens many artists because, unlike in the life-class, your subject will not stay still while you sketch!

Drawing people in their environment is not easy, which is why I draw people most when I have 'captive' models, such as those waiting in airports. Recently I had the misfortune to use four American airports in one day – so I had a wealth of subjects to sketch! There is always a variety of people of all ages, talking, reading, sleeping or just sitting around. Sketch quickly without inhibition and don't worry about mistakes. Don't destroy the mistakes – leave them to remind you why the sketch went wrong.

Church dignitary, Winchester: felt pen, 5 × 2 in (128 × 50 mm)

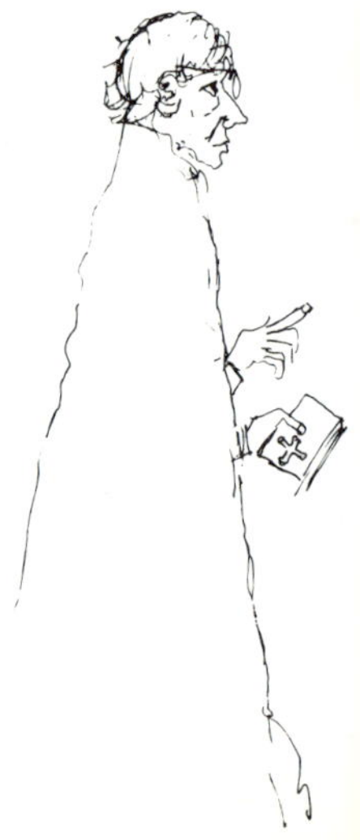

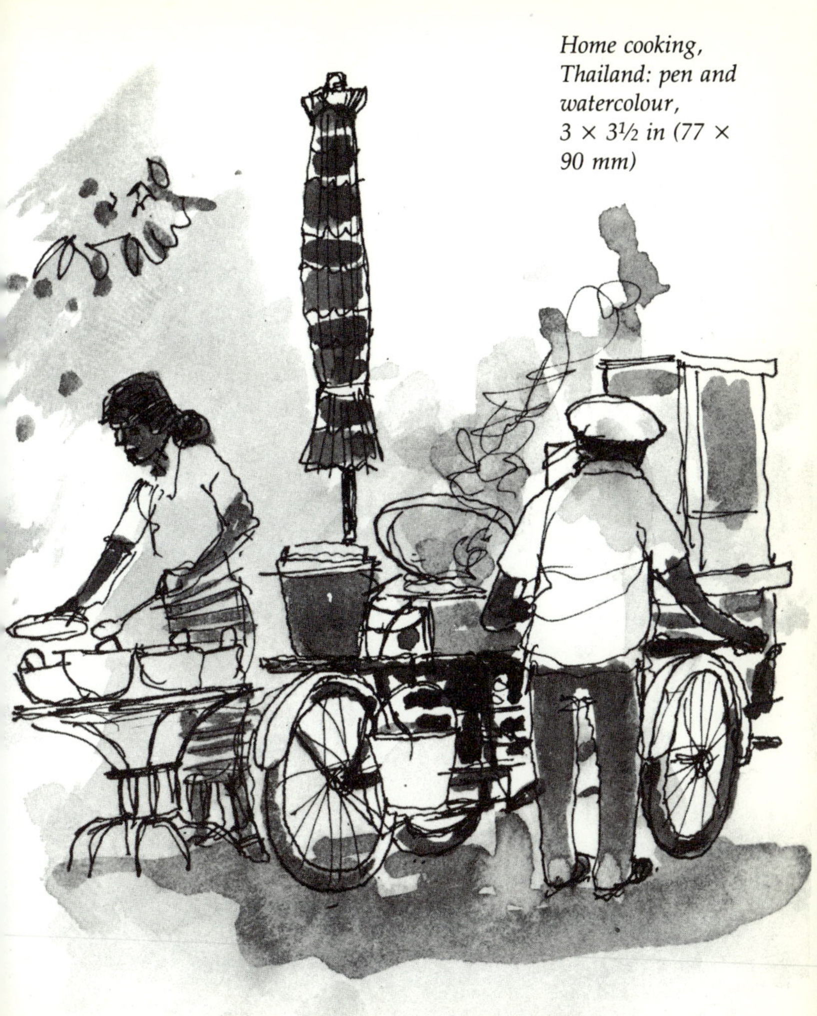

Home cooking, Thailand: pen and watercolour, 3 × 3½ in (77 × 90 mm)

St Louis Airport, USA: felt pen, S/S

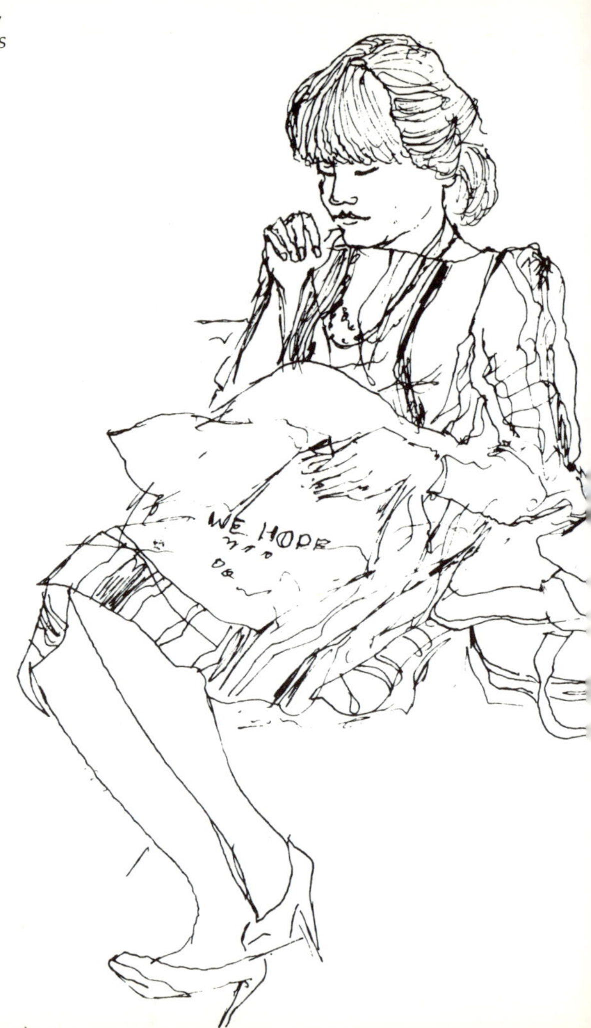

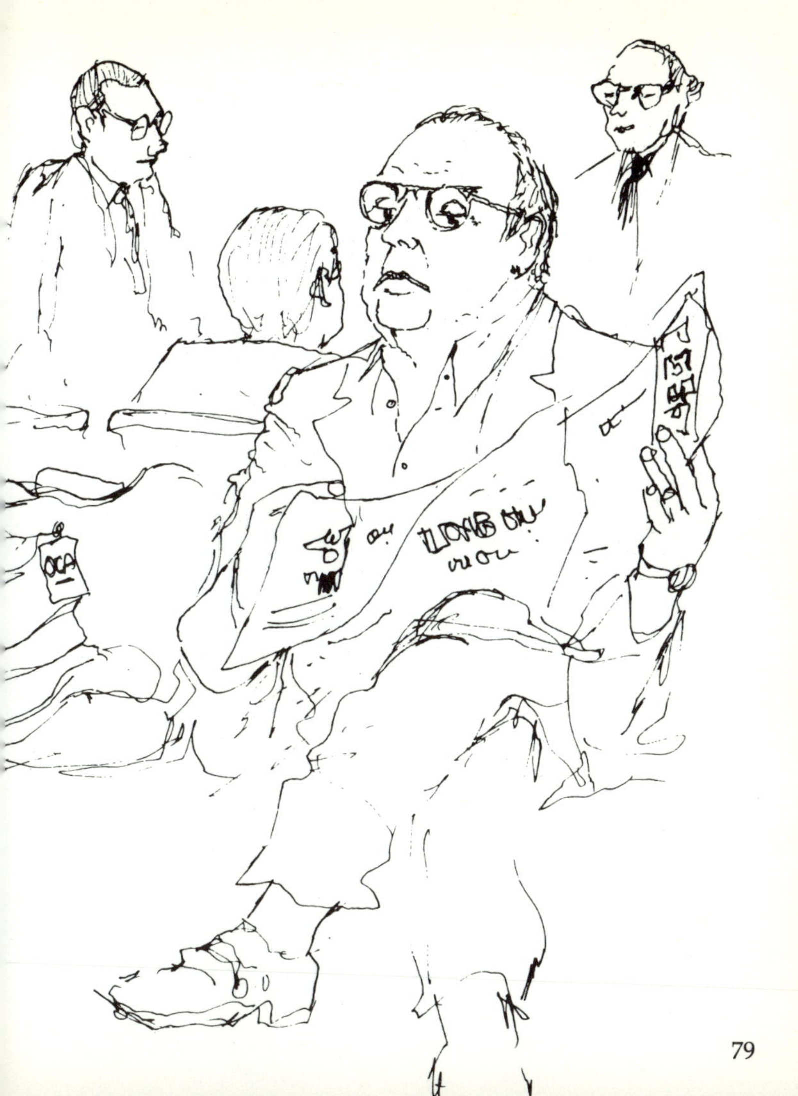

I always start with the head and then move on to the overall shape of the body and the all-important hands. If the person moves, try to wait until they return to something like the original position. One point to remember

OPPOSITE *Sketchbook figures: pen and watercolour,* S/S

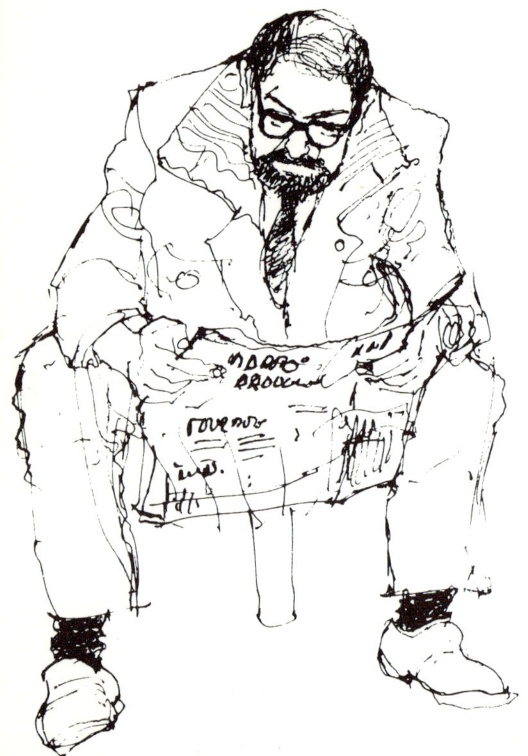

Newspaper reader, Heathrow Airport: Pilot techpoint pen $4\frac{1}{2} \times 3$ in (115 × 77 mm)

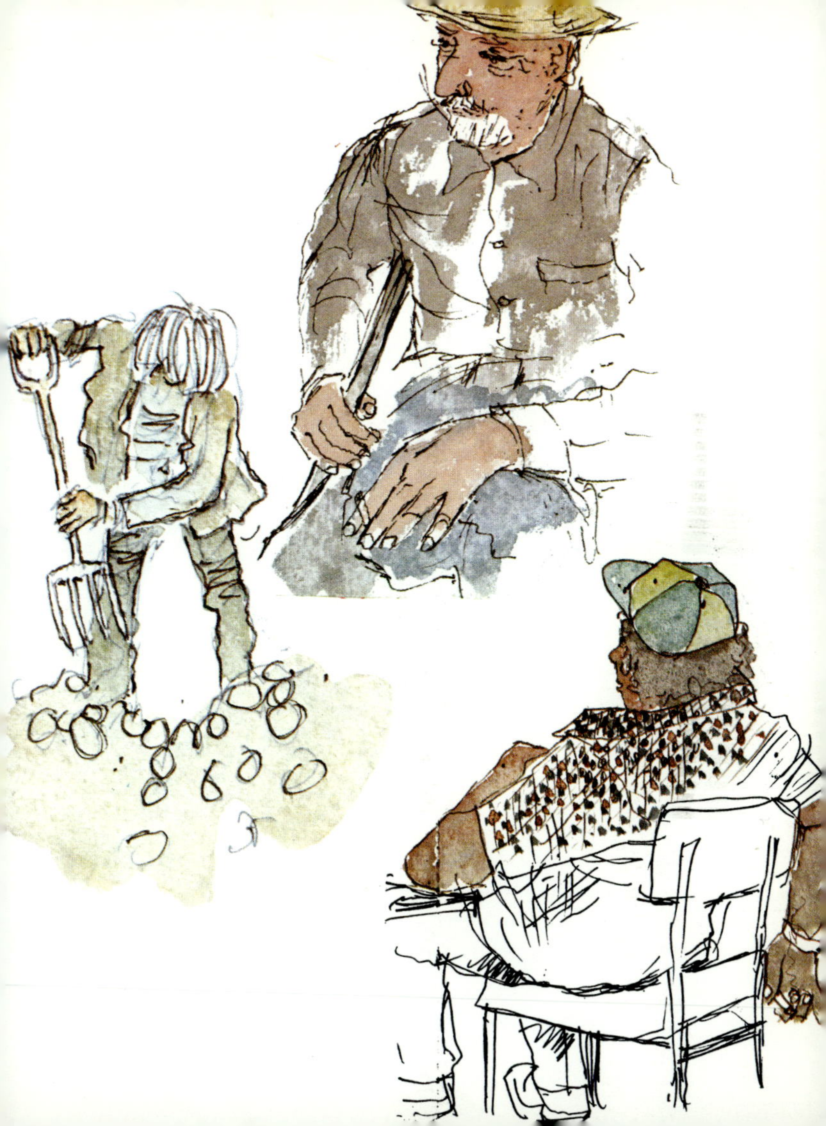

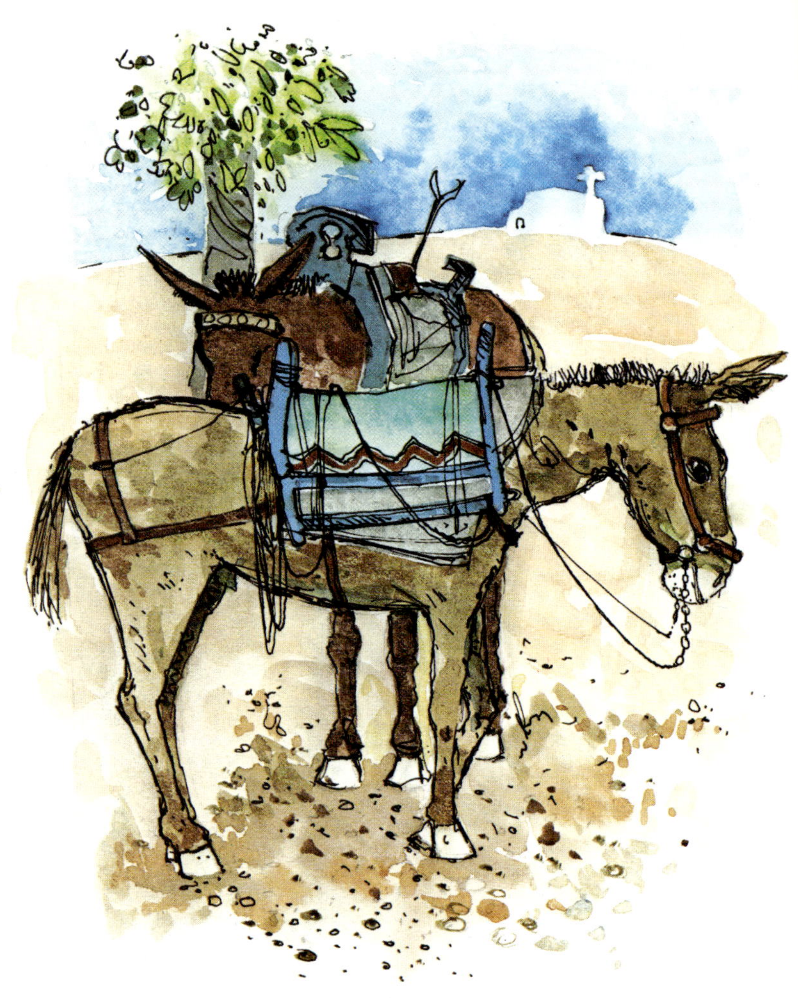

OPPOSITE *Greek mules: pen and watercolour,* S/S

is that the eyes come about half-way down the head, which may seem obvious, but a lot of people make the mistake of putting them too high up. Hands are notoriously difficult to draw but they do express character and emotion, so keep practising them.

When sitting sketching it is great fun to try to avoid being spotted. You can become quite cunning and if I am spotted by my subject I pretend that I am drawing someone else.

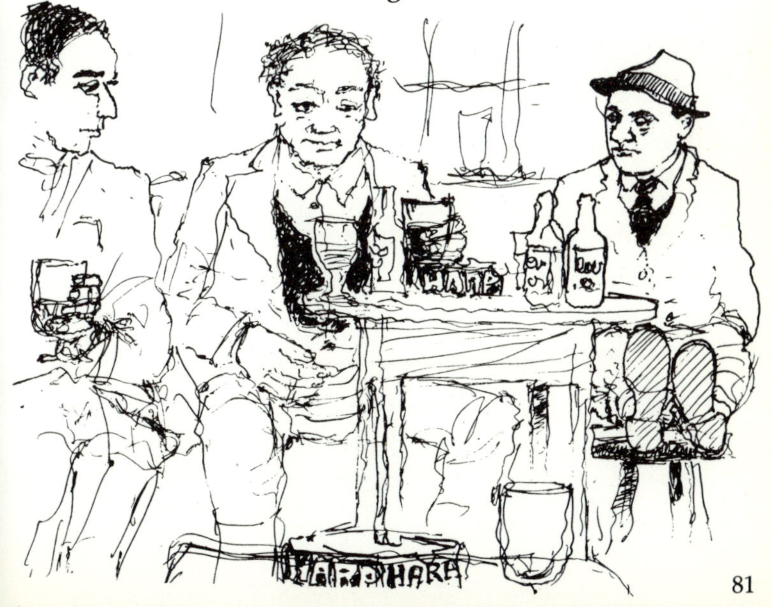

Cornish pub: technical pen, 5 × 4 in (128 × 100 mm)

Drawing animals is often a bit easier, because although they move about a lot, they have no idea that they are being sketched, so are quite uninhibited!

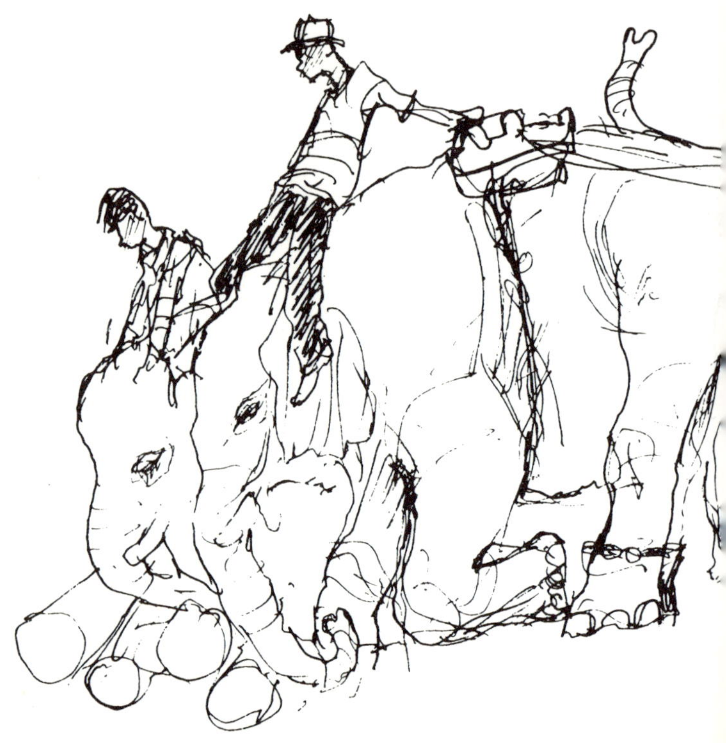

I found these elephants very exciting and challenging to draw – they were not as easy as I had first imagined. Although they are lumbering and slow-moving it was this majes-

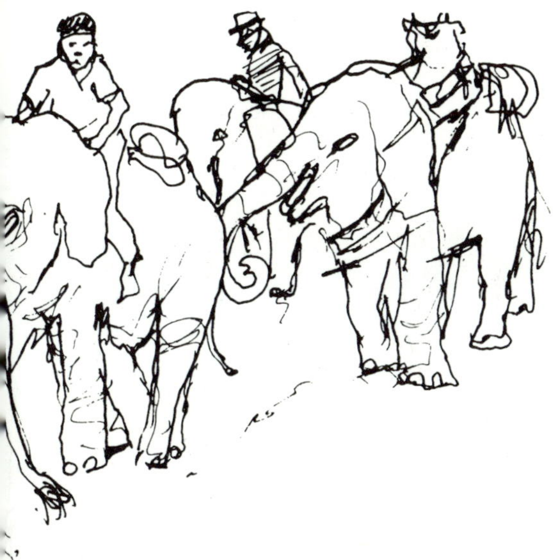

Working elephants, Thailand: fountain pen, s/s

tic ponderousness which was difficult, yet essential, to express. It helped having the drivers sitting on them to lend a sense of scale to the drawing.

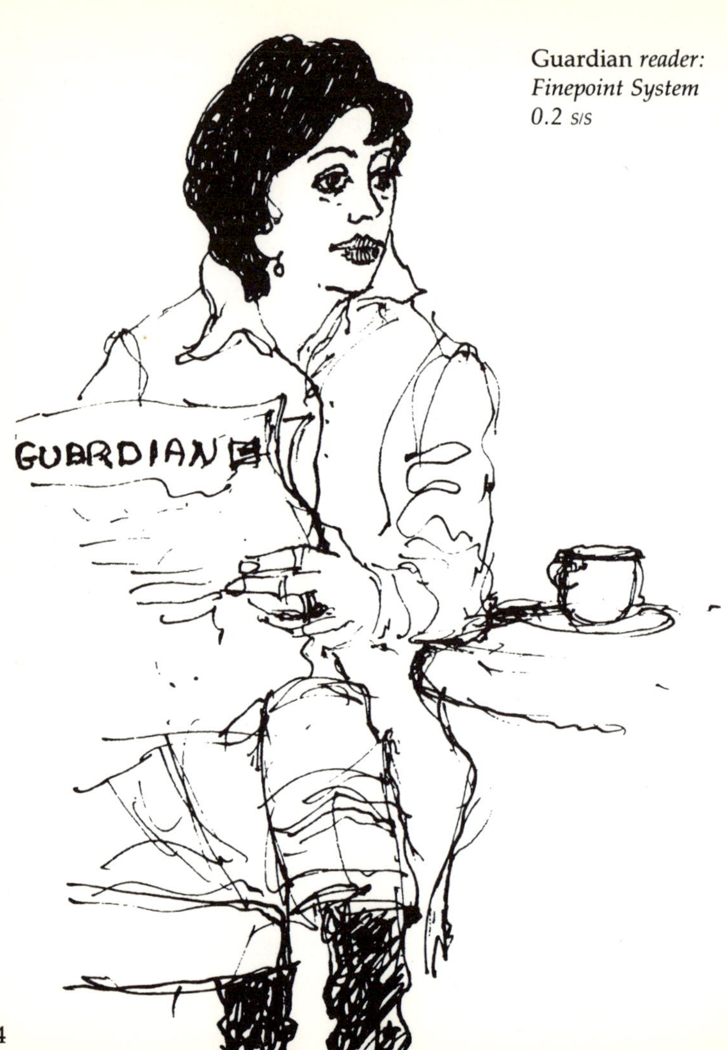

Guardian *reader:*
Finepoint System
0.2 s/s

You must draw animals quickly as they are always on the move, but look hard at their anatomy and bone structure. You need constant practice with lots of quick sketches to become proficient. I find that watercolour, line and wash, and simple line are the most effective media to use so that you do not have to worry too much over technique. A field of cows or sheep, a zoo or safari park are good places to begin because when one animal moves away, another will probably take up almost the same position.

Don't be disheartened by failure when drawing people and animals, but keep trying – it is not easy but very rewarding. I often do a drawing I am not satisfied with, but there are other times when it comes out well and captures all the feeling and emotion I felt when looking at the subject. Try not to overwork your drawing as a quick sketch often catches the essence of the animal or person much better. Don't worry too much about likeness – concentrate on lively drawings with good proportions.

Mother, Bangkok: technical pen, S/S

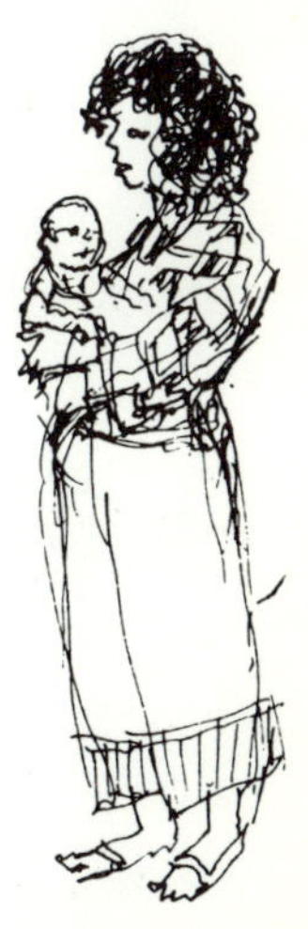

TREES

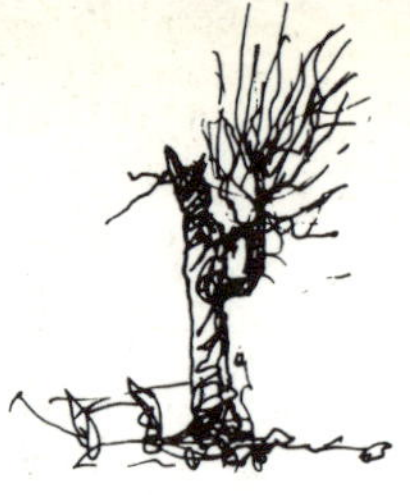

Trees are an integral and important part of any landscape. They contribute to the overall pattern made by hills, walls, fences, hedges, roads, farms and villages.

Izaak Walton Tree: technical pen, 4½ × 3½ in (115 × 90 mm)

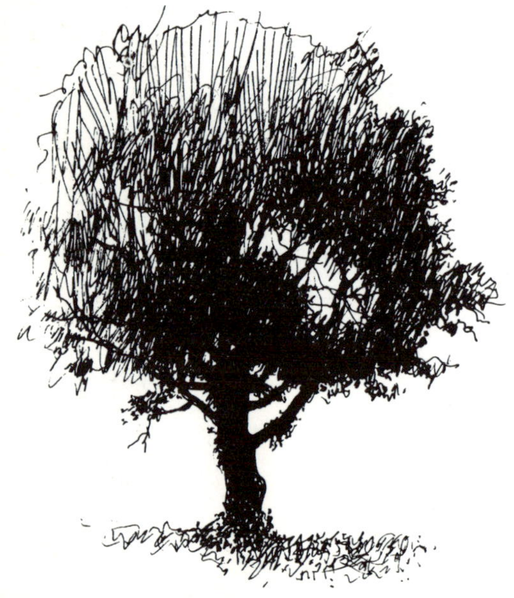

OPPOSITE
Mojácar, Spain: pen with 303 nib, 8½ × 6 in (215 × 152 mm)

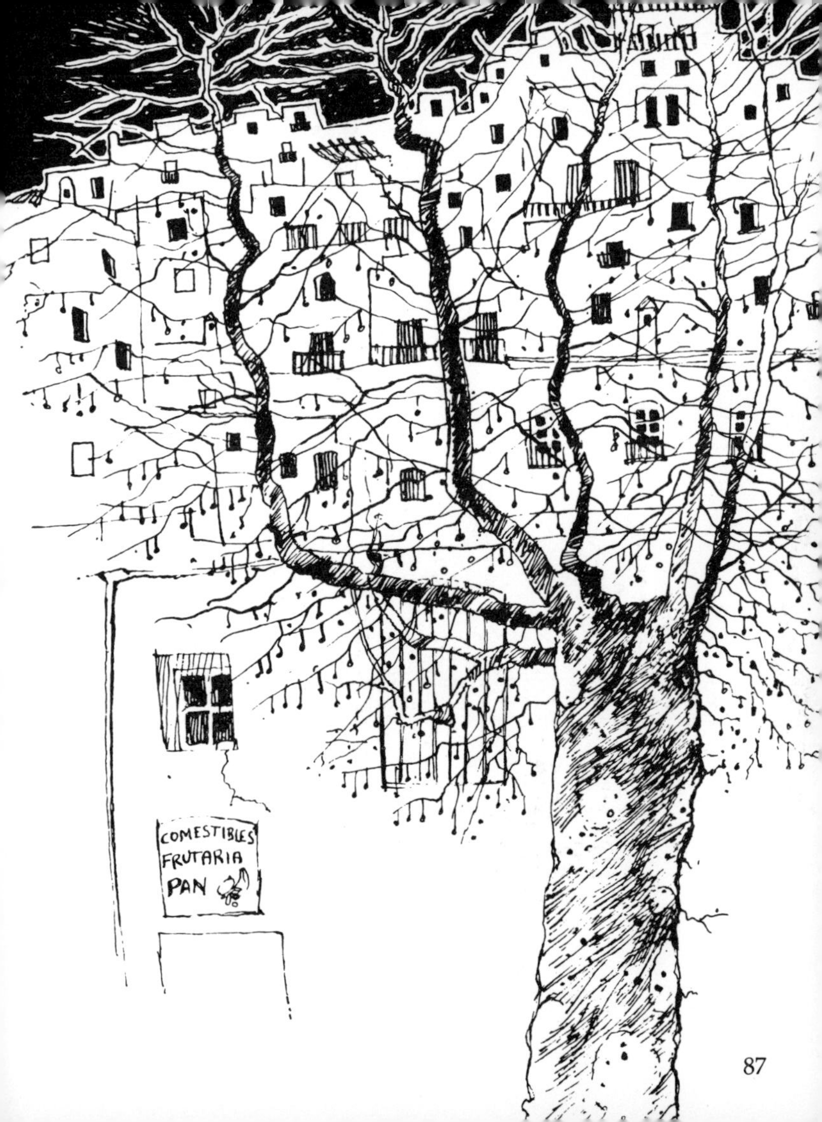
COMESTIBLES
FRUTARIA
PAN

For me, bare, deciduous, winter trees are particularly beautiful in the way that they make wonderful stark traceries against the skyline and are such fine subjects for line and water-colour. From their bare winter skeletons you can see the shapes the trees will eventually take on in the summer.

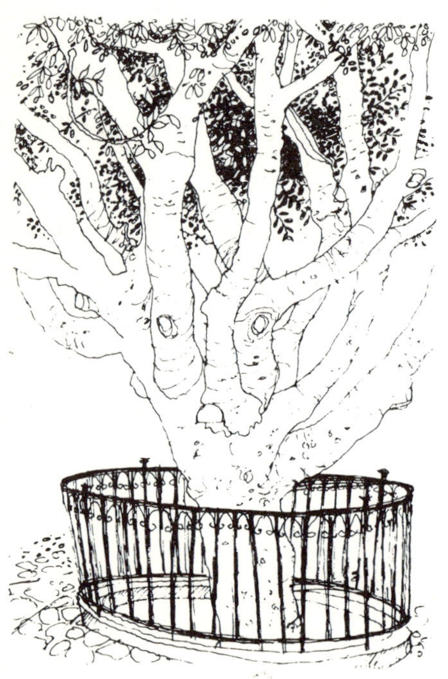

Tree in Mojácar, Spain: technical pen, S/S

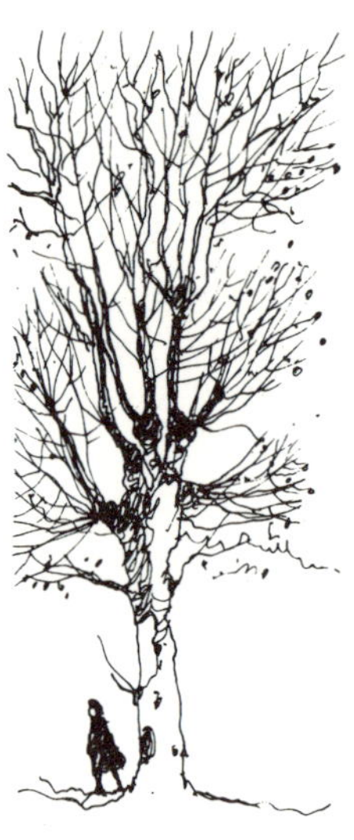

Tree in Pyrenees: Pygma pen 0.1, 5½ × 2 in (140 × 50 mm)

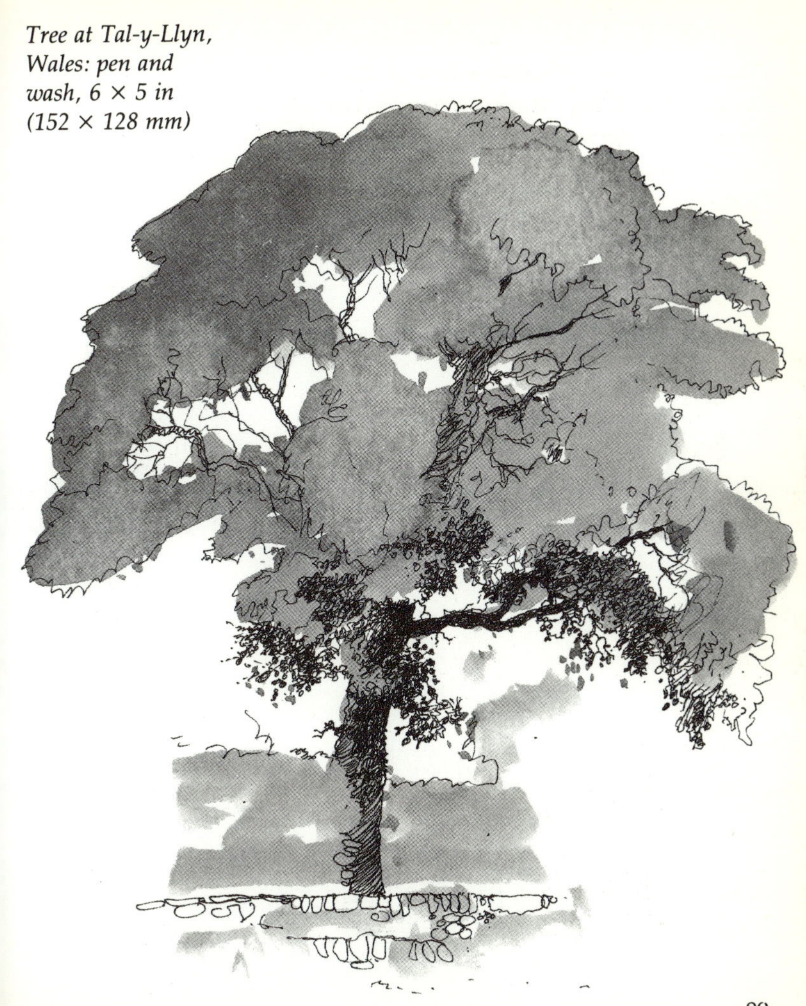

Tree at Tal-y-Llyn, Wales: pen and wash, 6 × 5 in (152 × 128 mm)

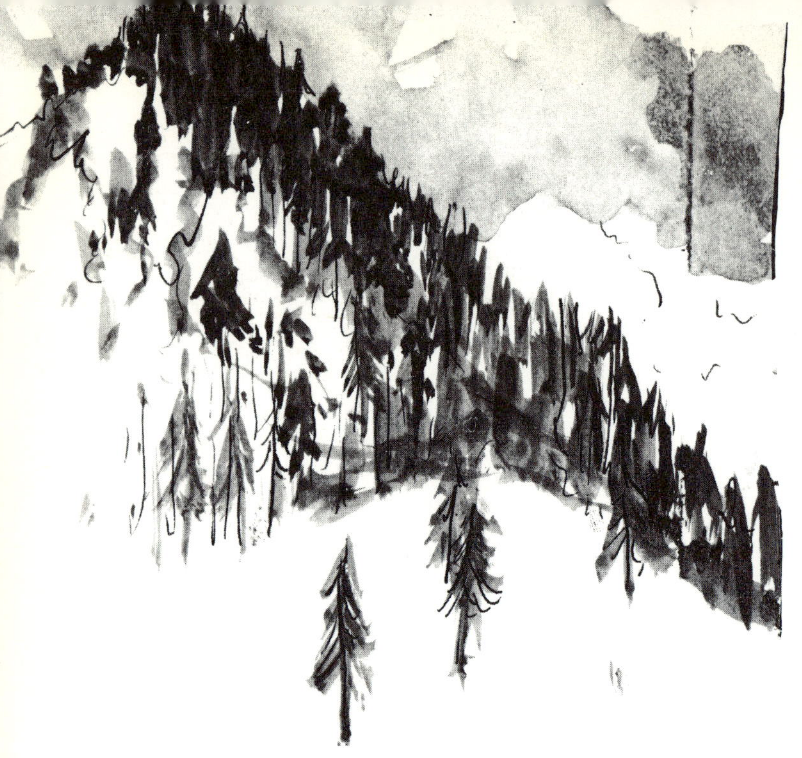

Fir trees, Romania: watercolour, S/S

Trees all have their own individual character; for example, fir trees always seem rather forbidding to me, especially in the snow, whereas I am very fond of the proud elm with its high 'waist' and always surrounded by a cloud of rooks.

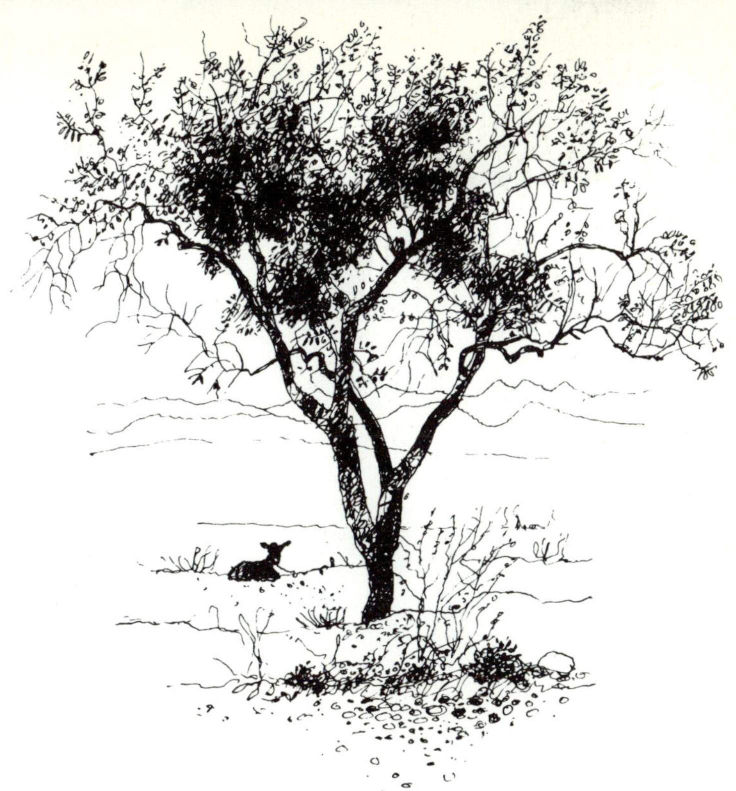

Olive tree near Turre, Almeriá: Rotring technical pen 0.25, 5 × 4½ in (128 × 115 mm)

I have included in this section many different trees that have interested me: the plane tree framing the box-like houses in southern Spain; the beautiful bush-like olive tree; the fir trees in the snow on the mountainside in Romania and an oak tree in summer.

BUILDINGS

Budapest: pen and ink, 4 × 5 in (100 × 128 mm)

Buildings are one of my favourite subjects, perhaps partly because of my early training in an architect's drawing office and also because it seems to me that buildings form an important part of our lives. There is a wealth of variety in the different buildings that surround us: houses, offices, farms, churches, museums and pubs. It gives me endless satisfaction when travelling abroad to look at buildings and to try to find out why they have been designed and built in the way they have, and to discover all the social and climatic factors involved.

Unfortunately, nowadays cities all over the world are beginning to resemble each other as traditional materials get more expensive to use and pre-stressed concrete becomes universal. Even so, certain building materials remain characteristic of particular parts of the world, such as Cotswold stone, Welsh slate, Spanish whitewashed stone, and Roman tiles. In the Far East the buildings often have wide overhangings and rooms open to the elements because of the high humidity, whereas in the Mediterranean they have shutters to keep out the sun that the English are only too anxious to let in!

OVERLEAF *Sorbas, Spain: pen and watercolour,* S/S

Dieppe, France: technical pen and wash, 5½ × 4 in (140 × 100 mm)

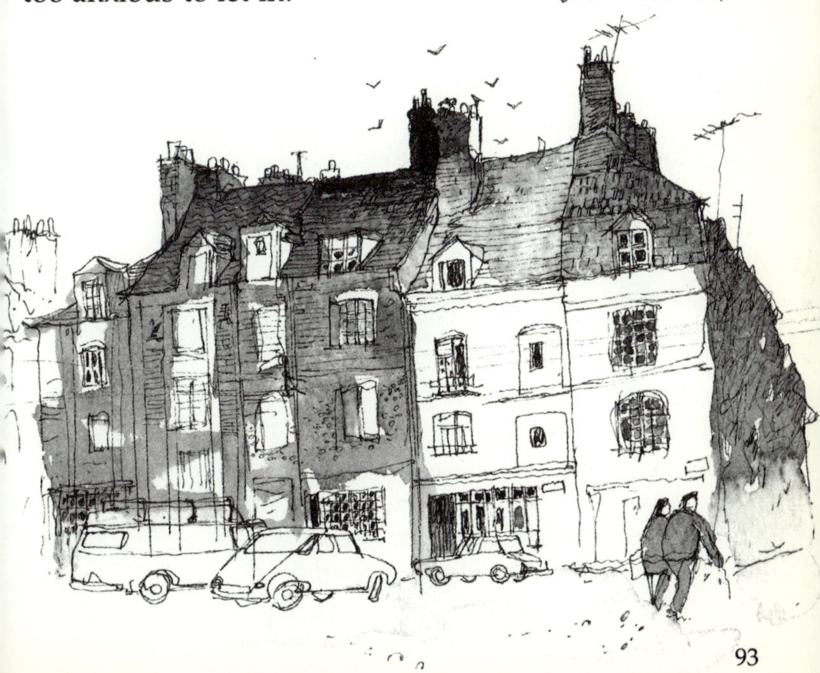

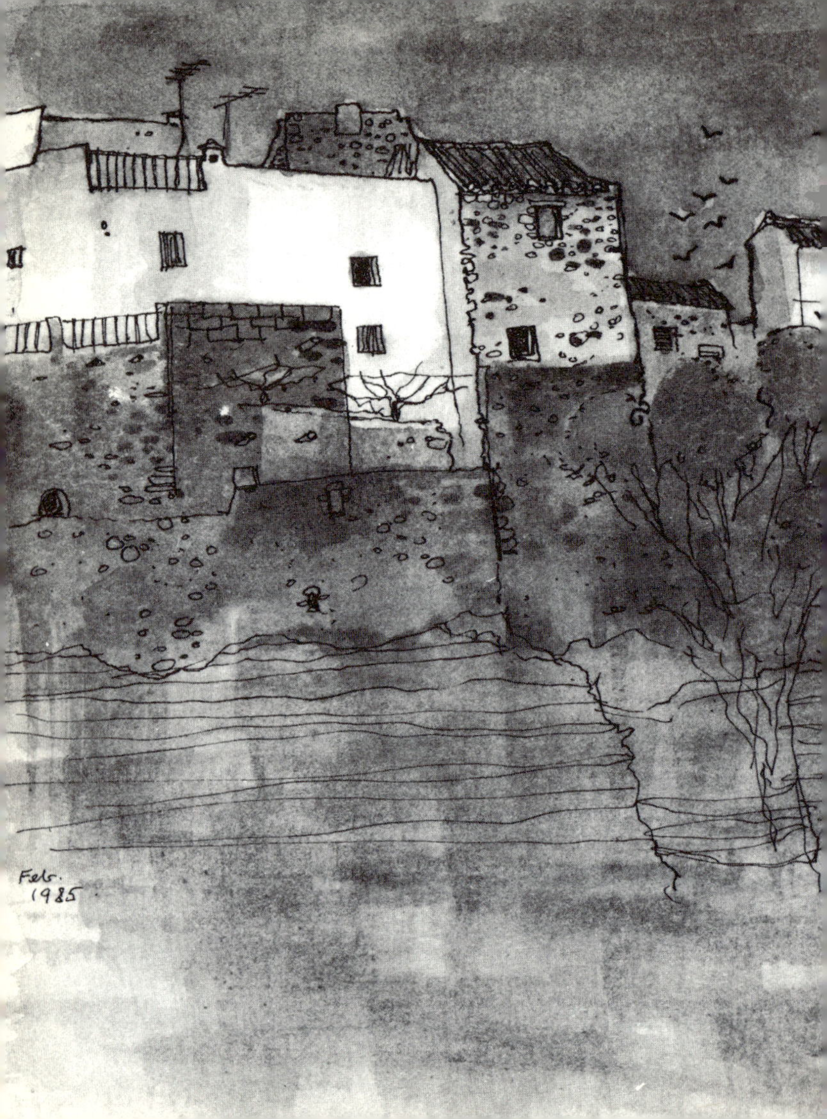
Feb.
1985

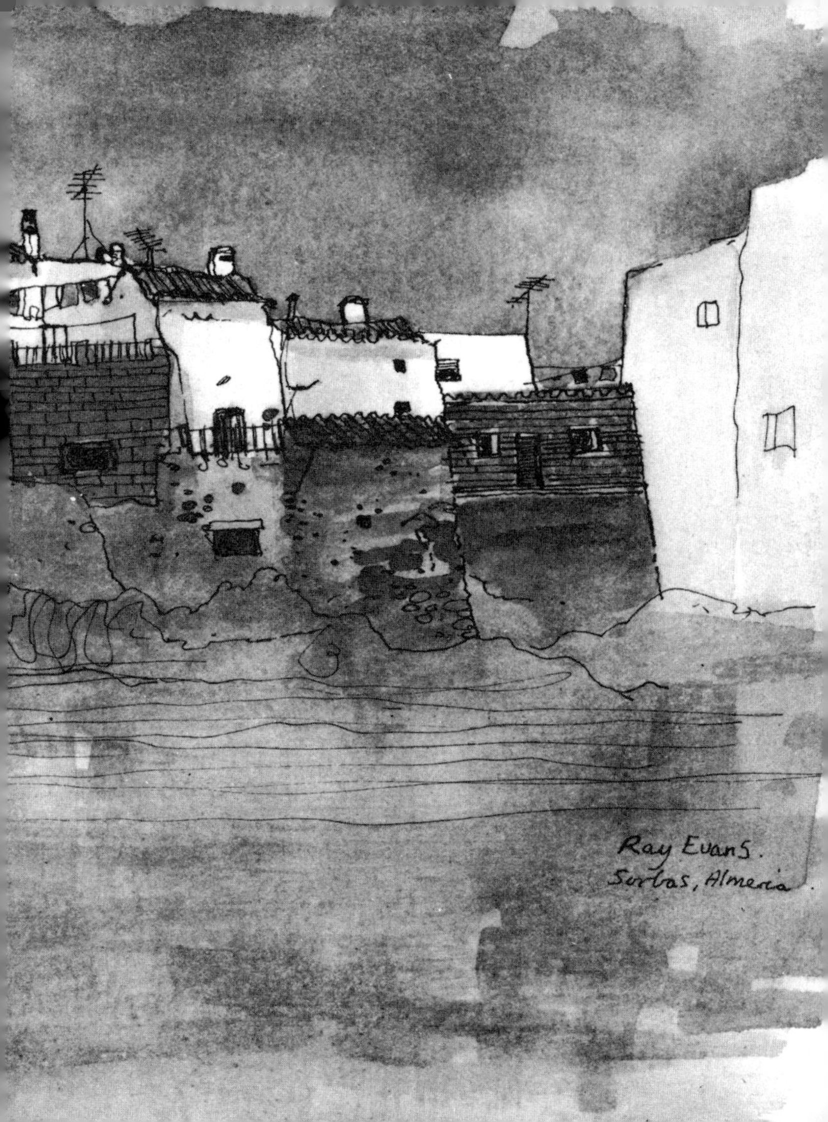
Ray Evans.
Sorbas, Almeria.

Towns and villages built on hill tops have always impressed me as they seem to be a natural extension of the landscape. I have always loved the cliff-hanging town of Sorbas in southern Spain on the previous page.

Many buildings like palaces, castles and cathedrals have recognizable functions, but it is the way in which they have been built that fascinates me, which is why a basic knowledge of architecture is helpful when drawing them, just as a knowledge of anatomy is useful when drawing the human figure.

OPPOSITE
Amsterdam: watercolour and pen, S/S

Much Wenlock: pen and wash, 6 × 4 in (152 × 100 mm)

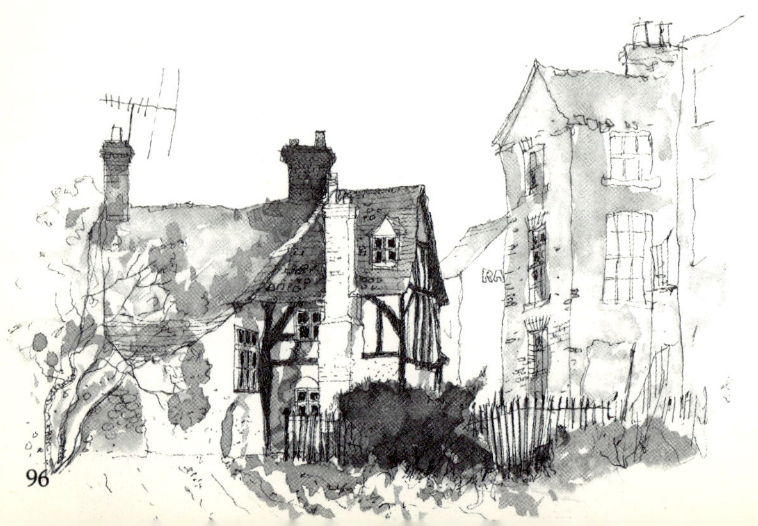

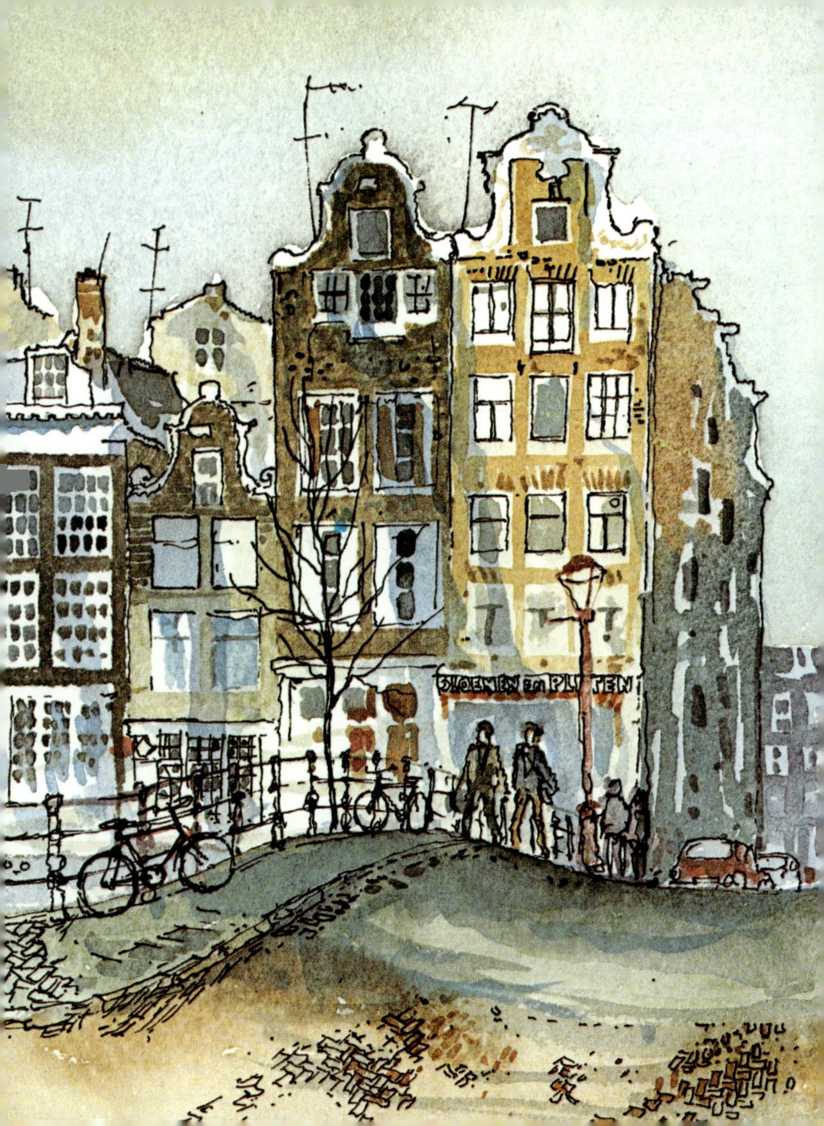
BLOEMEN en PL TEN

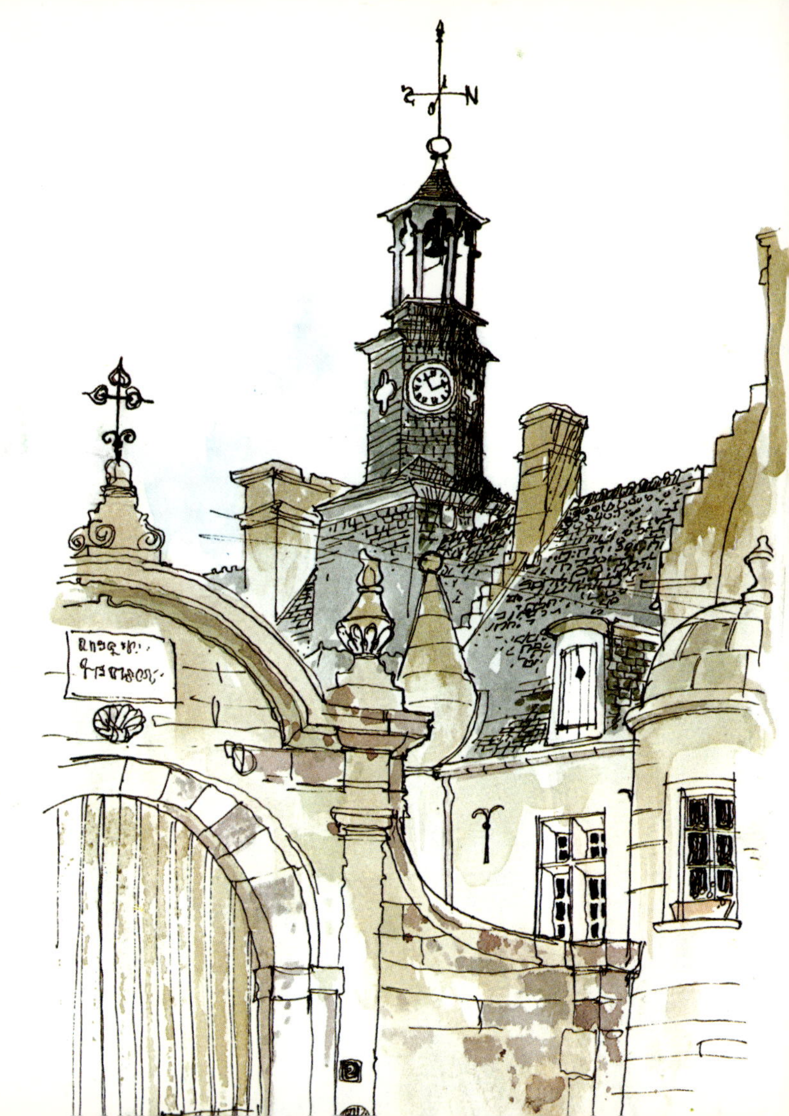

OPPOSITE
French château: watercolour and pen, $8\frac{1}{2} \times 5$ in (215 × 128 mm)

Learn to 'read' old buildings by drawing them. You will soon discover which materials have been used in their construction. If I cannot deduce what materials were used for the building when I look at a drawing or a painting of a building then there is something wrong with the drawing.

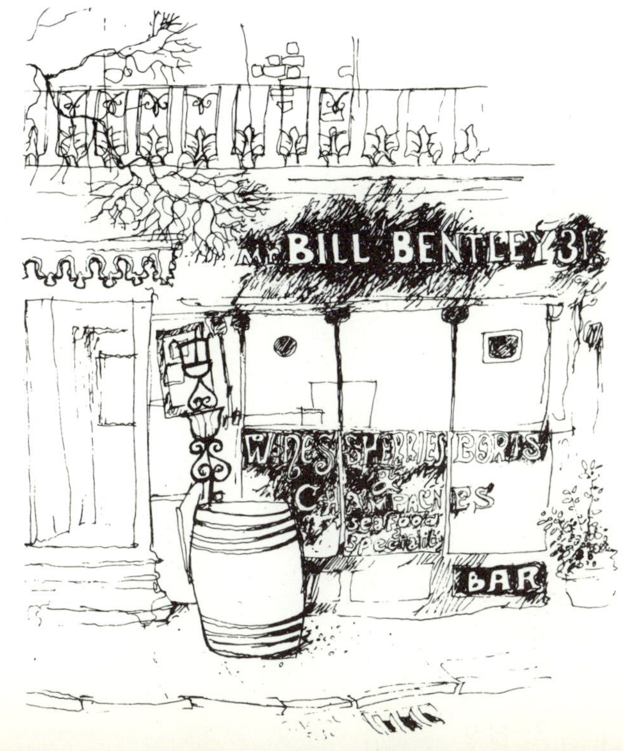

Bill Bentley Wine Bar, London: technical pen, S/S

OBSERVATION

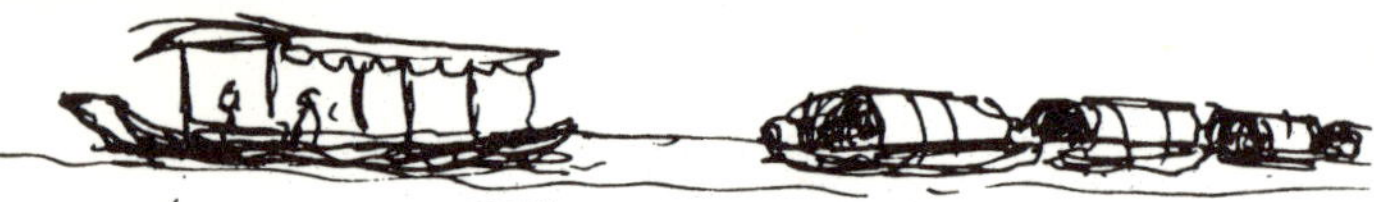

This chapter should be sub-titled 'noting and drawing'. It is always useful to make written notes on, or beside, the drawings you do in your sketchbook. In this way you will not forget the details of what you have sketched and will get a great deal of pleasure in looking back through your sketchbooks over the years, if the drawings are dated, have place-names and other relevant details. It is also

OPPOSITE
Typical sketchbook page: Pilot H. Techpoint, S/S

Sleeping cat, fountain pen, 6 × 3½ in (152 × 90 mm)

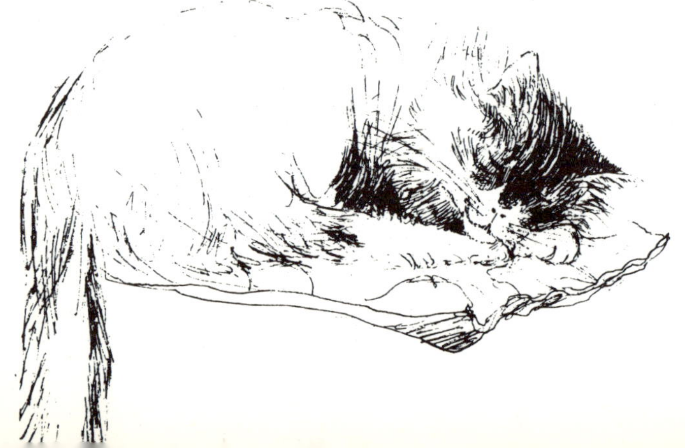

Start of Bangkok trip.
Drinking Bourbon in the Taverna
Coffee House at Heathrow

Staying at the
Crest Hotel
for night.
going up to
our room to watch
last "Manor Born"
Serial.

Diner reads
book

[illegible]
waiter

another young
diner reads
& eats his
dinner

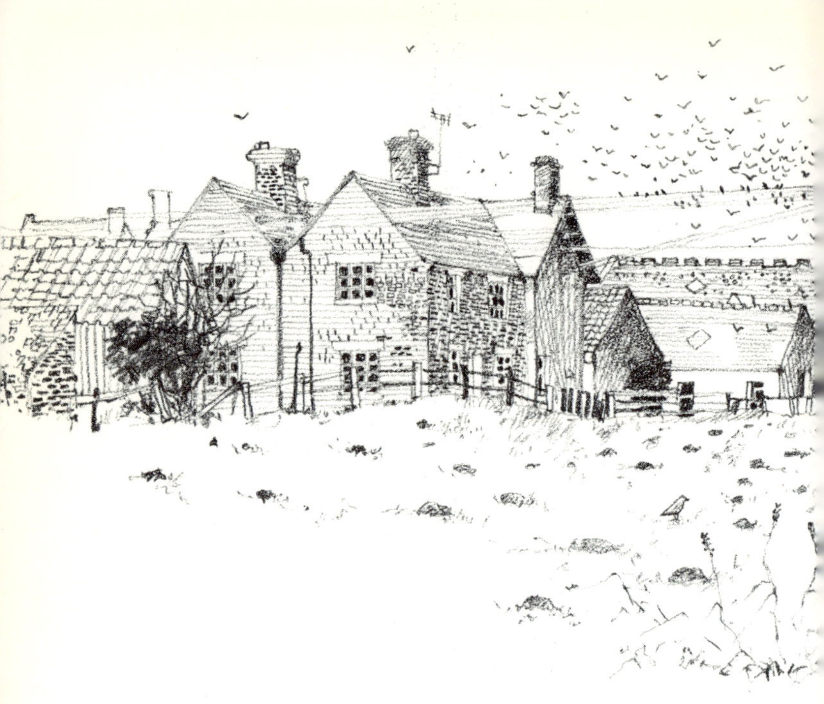

very important to make note of the type of drawing tool you have used.

I certainly could not have produced this book without the help of all the information I noted in my sketchbooks over the years!

All the drawings in this section are taken from small pocket sketchbooks,

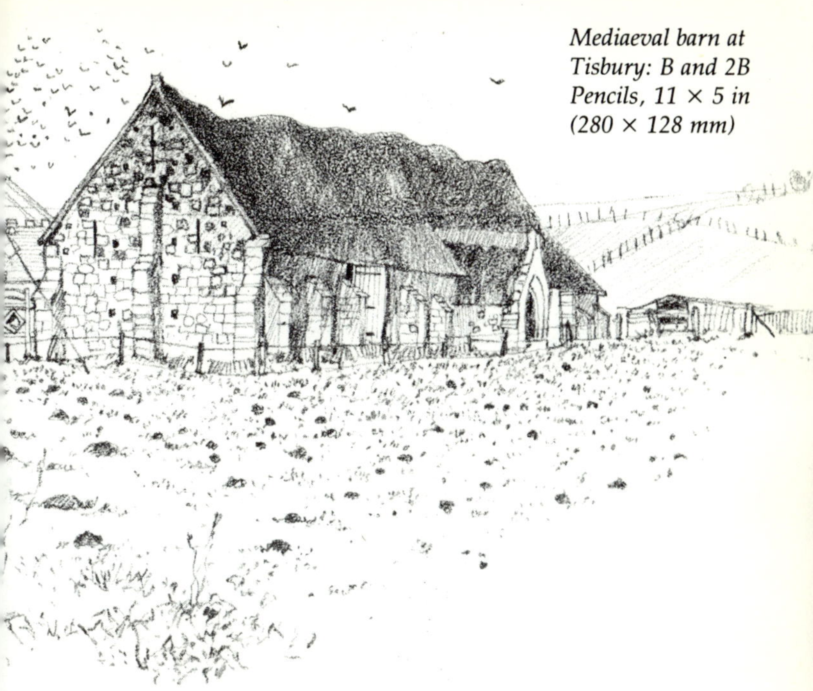

Mediaeval barn at Tisbury: B and 2B Pencils, 11 × 5 in (280 × 128 mm)

with the exception of the pencil drawing of the mediaeval barn at Tisbury above, which was drawn over a period of 1½ hours, on a board with a rough textured watercolour surface.

It is important to know what to look for when you start drawing. It is certainly easier to draw a subject which you find interesting and exciting, but a good composition can sometimes transform a rather ordinary subject into something quite extraordinary and you should try every point of view and angle before abandoning a subject. By framing your subject through the branches of a tree,

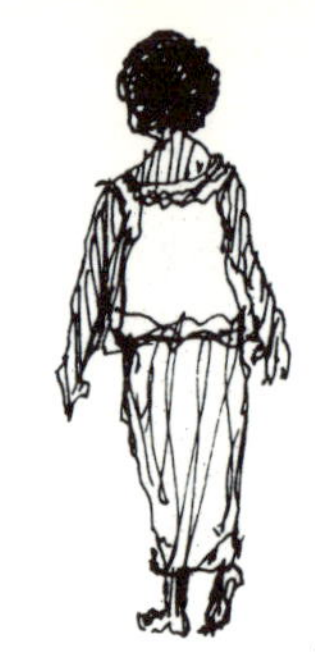

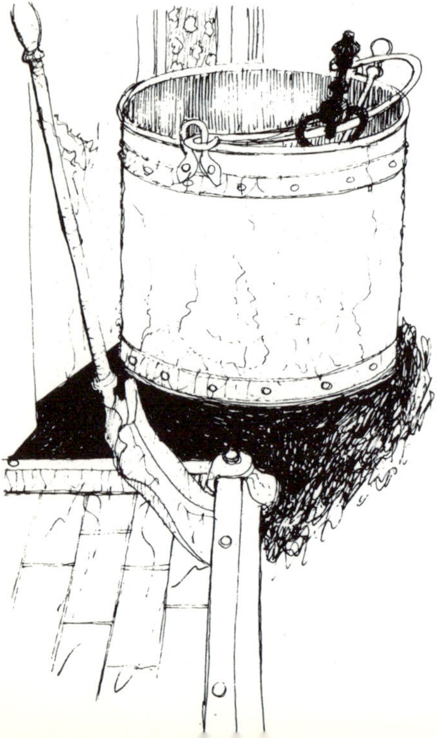

Hearth drawing: technical pen, S/S

through a window or with a close foreground, a new dimension can often be achieved. So it is worth observing carefully everything around you and trying to get into the habit of doing this.

It could be a very simple scene – a black cat asleep in the sun against a

Irish cottage: Gillott pen nib, 303, 6 × 3 in (152 × 77 mm)

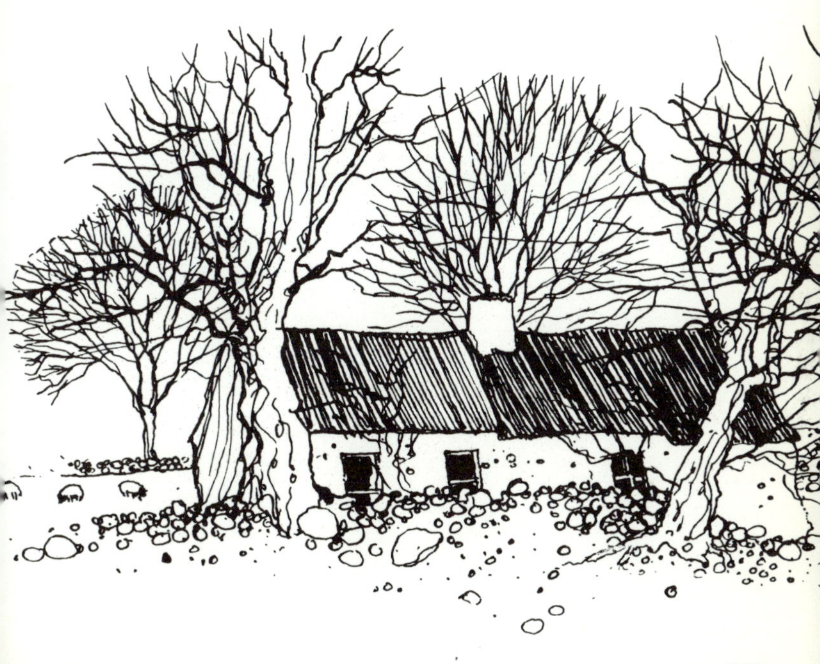

white door, or a view through shutters, a chair with a shadow cast by the sun, or chickens in a yard, seen through an open door. Take note of what's around you and then set your scene as a film director would, always leading the eye to the most interesting part of your drawing.

Big Sky Cowboys, Wyoming, USA: fountain pen, 3½ × 4½ in (90 × 115 mm)

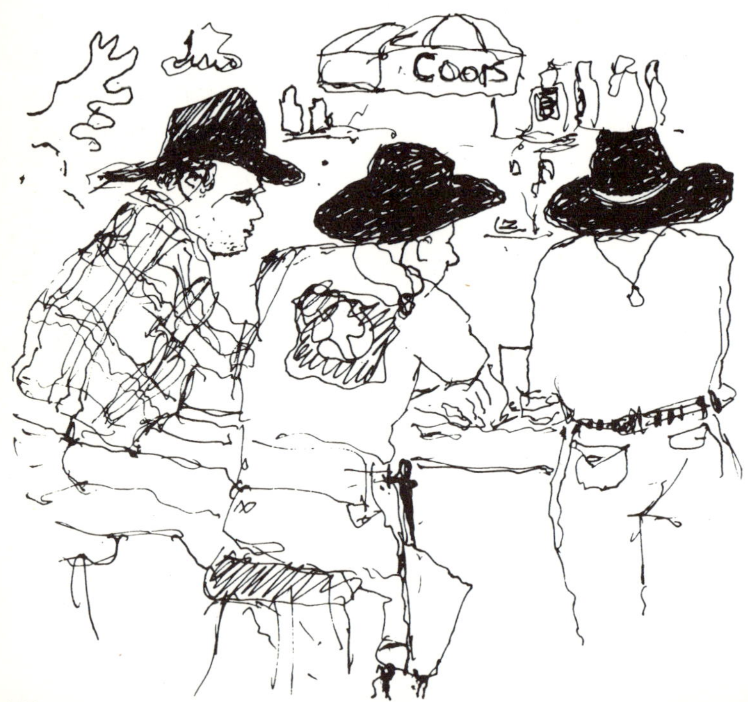

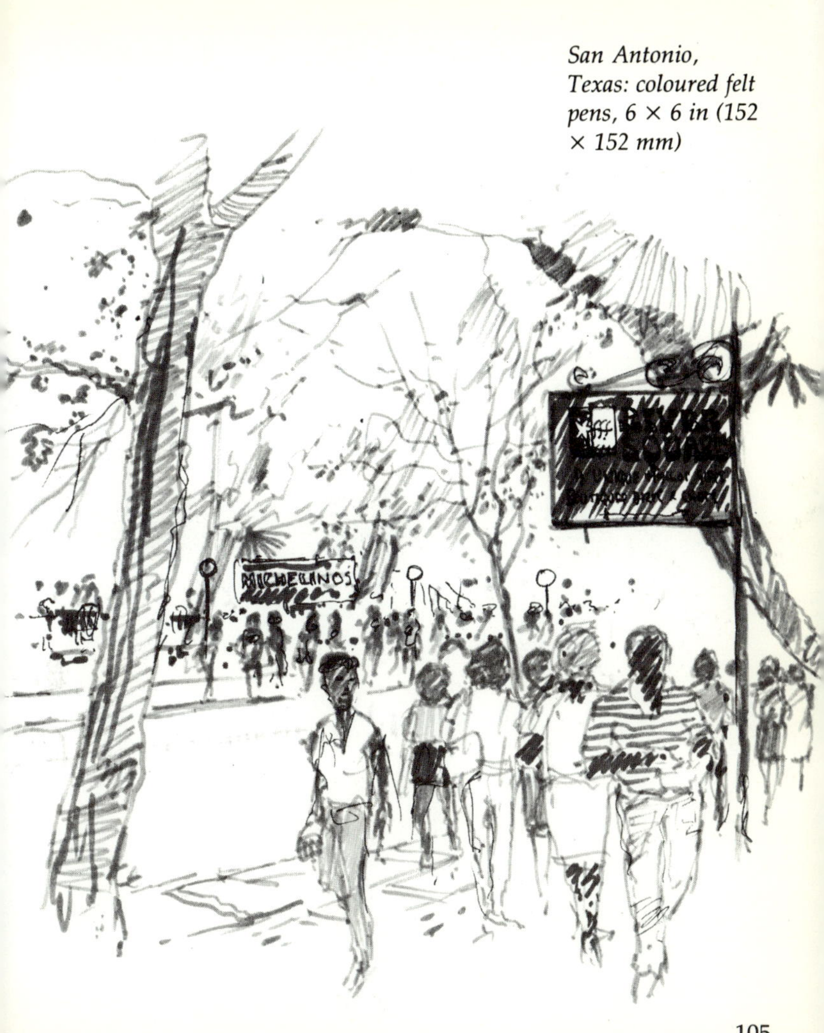

San Antonio, Texas: coloured felt pens, 6 × 6 in (152 × 152 mm)

INVENTION AND EXPERIMENT

Once we have learned to observe, the next step is to train ourselves to invent new and original ways of expressing things visually. You may ask how we can be original in this day and age when it seems that everything has been said and done before. After the genius of Michelangelo and the originality of Picasso where can we go? In fact, what is important is to try to express, without inhibition, your own feelings when looking at a particular scene.

I have tried to show with the illustrations in this section how we can view subjects with fresh eyes, and avoid the pitfall of beginning to copy ourselves all the time. Many professional artists find this a problem, especially where they have developed a certain style that is commercially successful.

OPPOSITE *Parador Nacional, Spain: Pilot H. Techpoint, S/S. This was drawn with exaggerated perspective to make the building look even more impressive.*

OVERLEAF *Washing at Turre, Spain: watercolour and pen, 8 × 6 in (200 × 152 mm)*

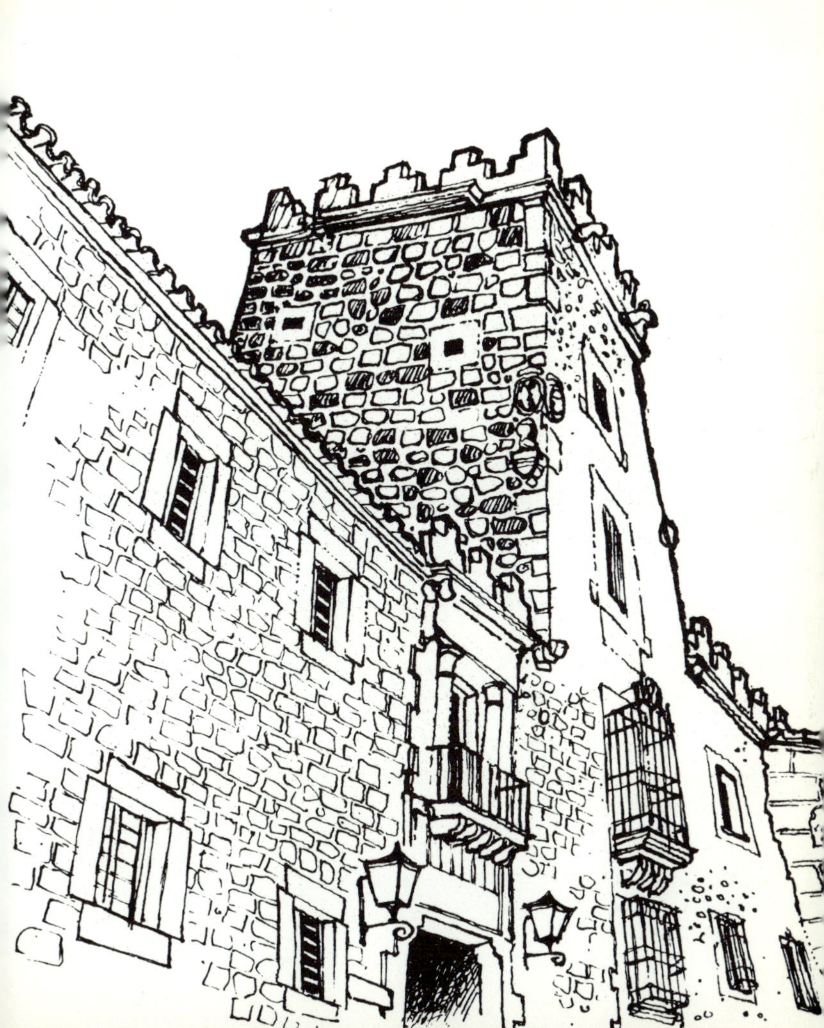

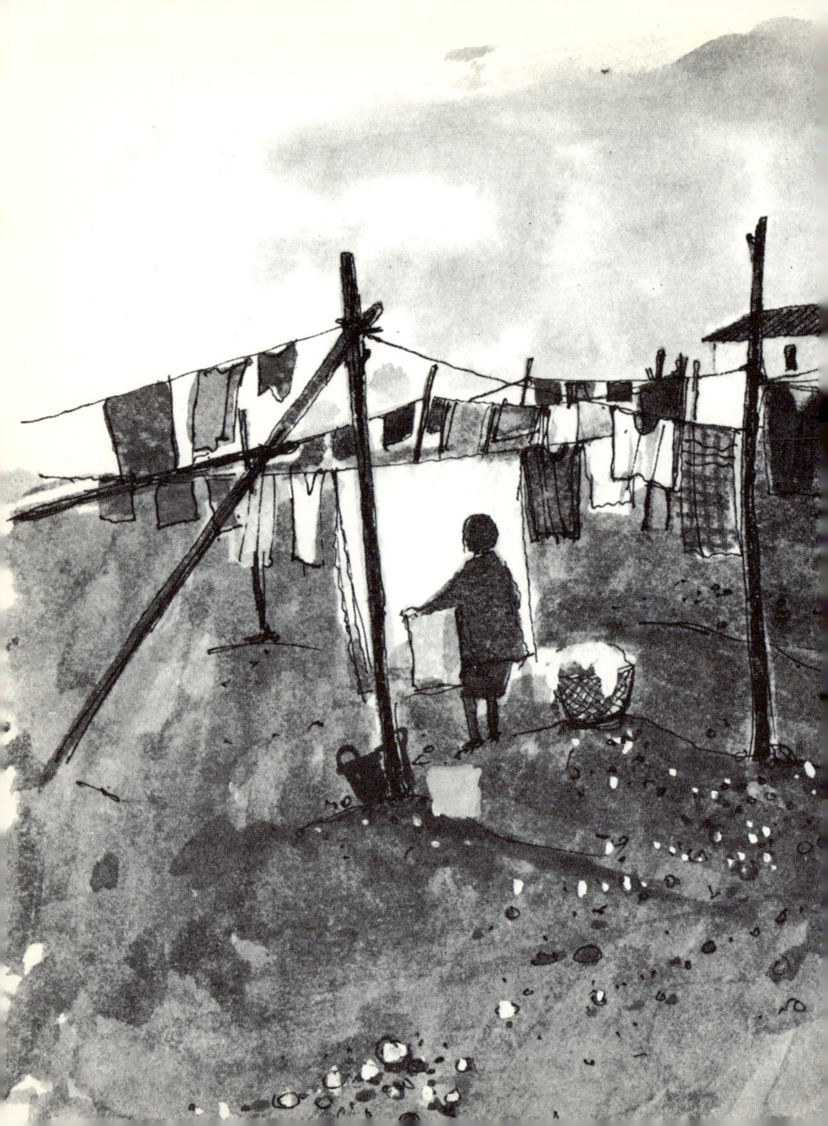

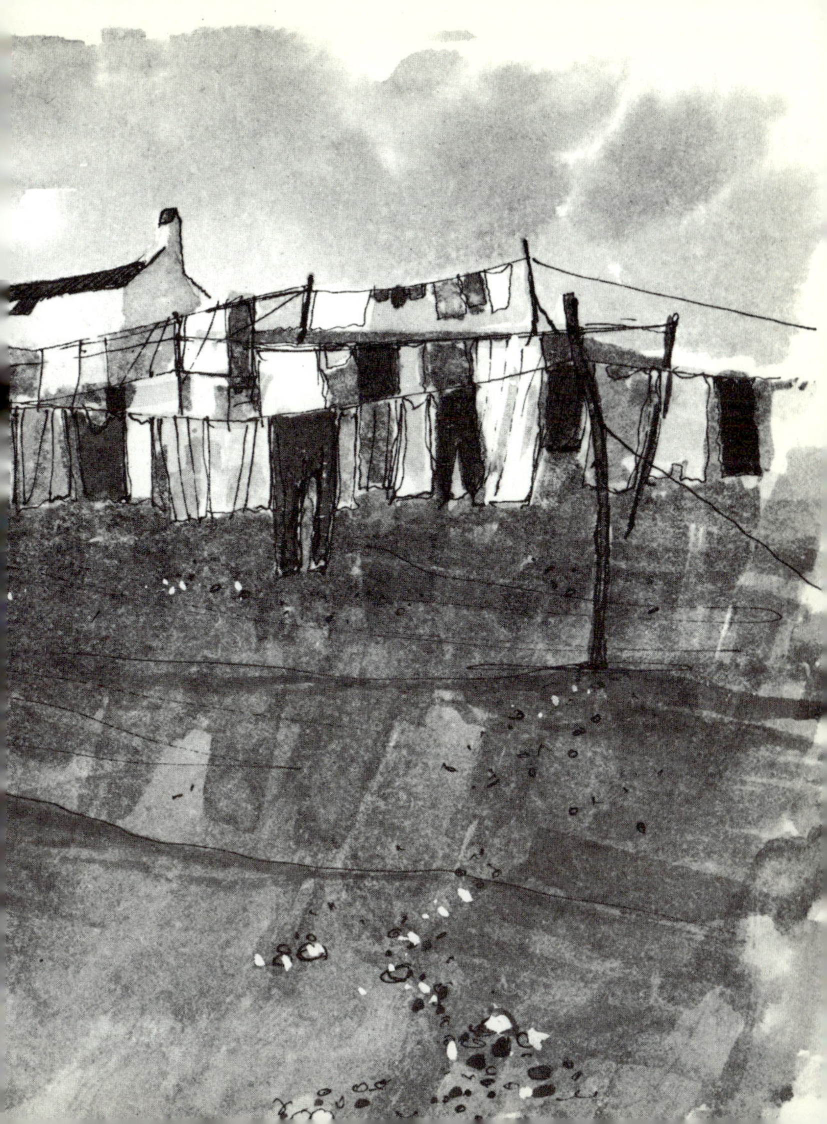

Take the drawing of 'Washing at Turre' on the previous page: I spotted the little chapel on the hill at the very top of the village of Turre in Spain. It was isolated and standing out white and rather stark against the blue of the sky. It was attractive but the foreground was bare, so I walked on around the hill and then I saw the washing, line upon line blowing in the breeze, and there was my foreground. It made a much more interesting drawing than if I had just sketched the chapel at first sight.

Within the limit of your sketchbook page you must consider the relationship of your work to that shape, particularly if you are making a finished sketch. It is within that framework that you can experiment to make the piece of work more original and interesting. Of course you may decide to alter the proportion of the page: I have had sketchbooks made up to different shapes. One favourite was long and narrow, 8½ × 4 in (210 × 100 mm), so all the drawings had to be that shape too, which was interesting.

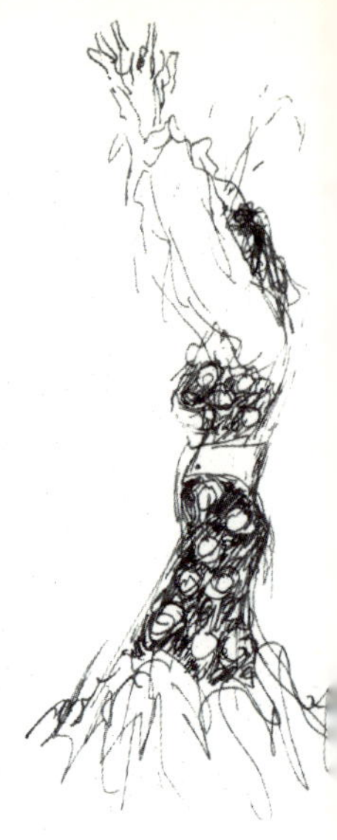

Spanish dancer: technical pen, 5 × 2 in (128 × 50 mm)

How exciting it is to go to a local art exhibition, and come across the occasional innovative piece of work. They are rare but there's usually something fresh and different to be found.

Try to be as original as possible in your composition and don't just copy the scene in front of you.

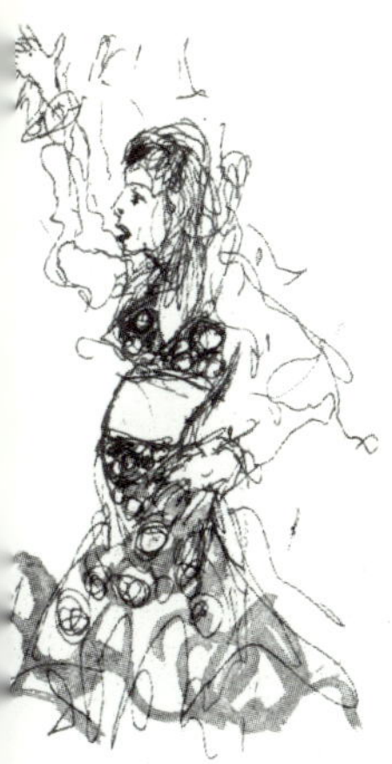

Spanish dancer: fibre tipped coloured pen, 5 × 3 in (128 × 77 mm)

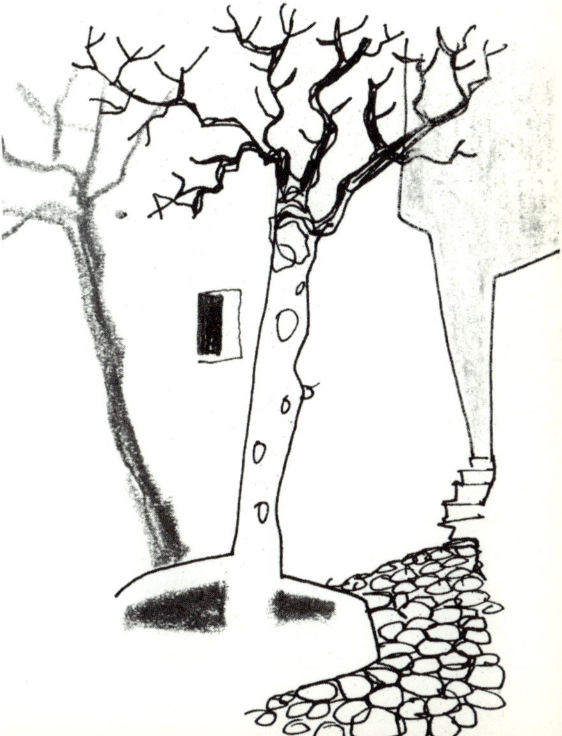

Landscape, Rhodes: pen and oil pastel, 4½ × 3½ in (115 × 90 mm)

PRACTICAL HINTS AND TIPS

I have covered most of the materials for sketching, such as pens, pencils, brushes and watercolours, in the Equipment and Materials chapter on pages 8–15. However, in this section I am just going to give you a few more hints and tips about other equipment.

If you are using pencils or crayons then you should always carry a sharp knife with you for sharpening them, and perhaps an eraser and some fixative. For most sketching I use a B pencil which does not need fixing, but if you use soft pencil or charcoal it will require fixing if you want to avoid the sketch smudging before you get home.

If you are going to work larger than this size pocket sketchbook then you will need to carry a sketching bag. A sketching bag should ideally have separate pockets for all the different items so that you can find what you

Leisure time, Paris: technical pen, 6 × 3½ in (152 × 90 mm)

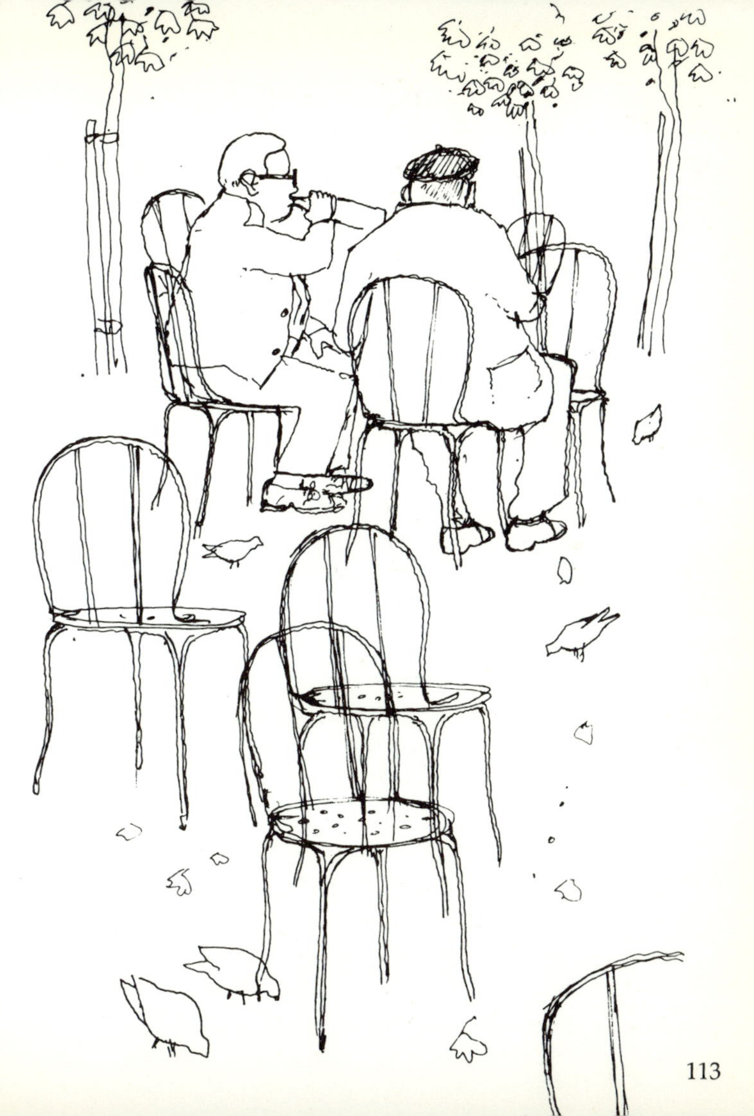

want quickly, and it should have a shoulder strap to facilitate carrying and be lightweight but strong. I take an easel and a larger folio when I am travelling by car. You will also want something to sit on – my favourite sketching stool is light, comfortable, has a walking-stick handle, and opens up like an armchair.

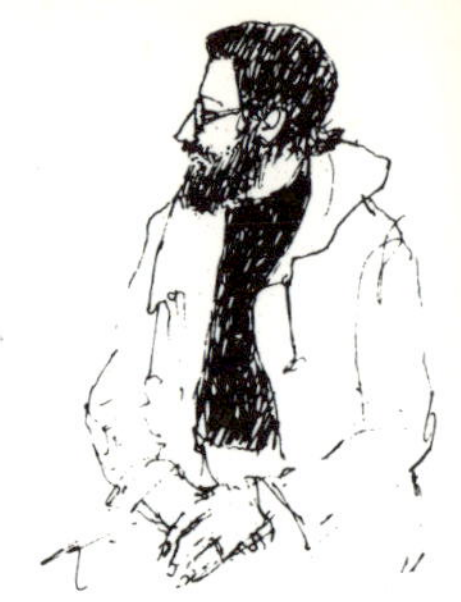

Customer in the King of Prussia pub: fibre tipped pen, 3 × 2 in (77 × 50 mm)

If I am using larger sketchbooks then I prefer the Daler-Rowney ones with Bockingford 140 lb watercolour paper, which is suitable for both pen and watercolour work. The sizes range from 7 × 5 in (180 × 125 mm) to 20 × 16 in (510 × 410 mm).

Once you are happy with your materials, you can concentrate on your sketching. Do remember though, that although I have tried to give you some useful guidelines to follow in this book, you have the artistic licence to bend the rules. After all, as the old proverb says, 'the exception proves the rule'. Sometimes a pencil drawing roughly sketched on the back of an envelope has a sparkle and verve that you wish you could always achieve.

Frenchman: fibre tipped pen, 4 × 3 in (100 × 77 mm)

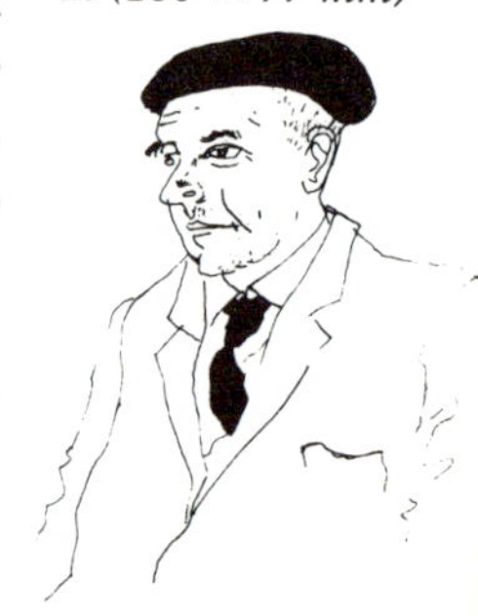

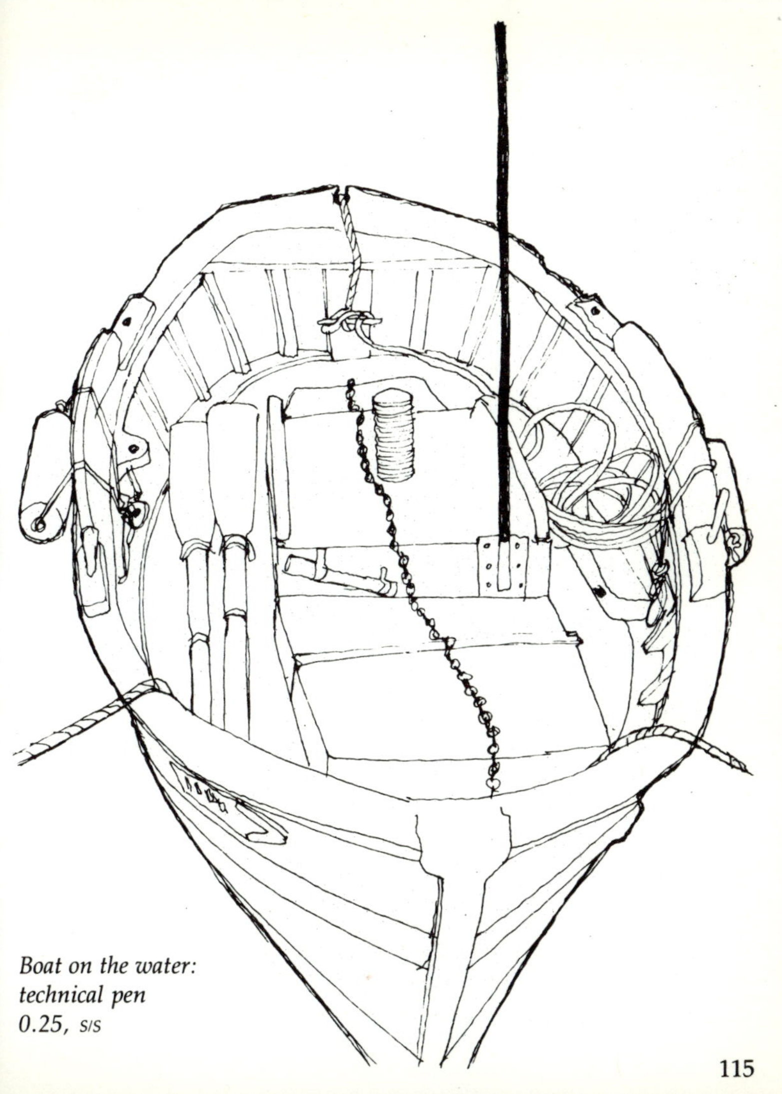

Boat on the water: technical pen 0.25, S/S

One of the most important things to remember is the limitation of your page area. However quick and spontaneous your sketch is you must get all the features into the area you are using so that the drawing doesn't run off the page. Gauge before you start whether it will fit the page – see my pen drawing on page 114 of a small fishing boat. The boat was lying flat in the water as I looked down on it from the quay where I was sitting. Other factors, such as the strength of line to

Overheard in a Chicago restaurant: 'That guy had his hi-fi on so loud you couldn't hear yourself think. The only way to stop him is to go in and bust his lip'; grey and black felt pens, S/S

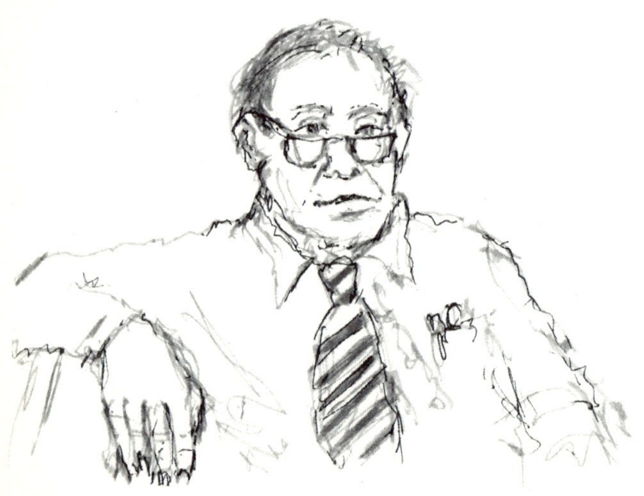

use, the tonal values, and perspective, will eventually become automatic and although important, are secondary to the subject matter and composition.

Before going out sketching do make a check list of all your favourite equipment. Refer to this list whenever you go out or are going away on a trip. It is very annoying to discover that you have left behind your favourite pen or brush and the village shop where you end up has never heard of a Gillott nib or a Rotring technical pen!

Street scene, Bangkok: technical pen, S/S

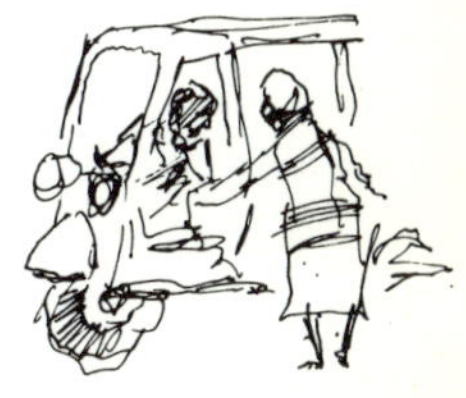

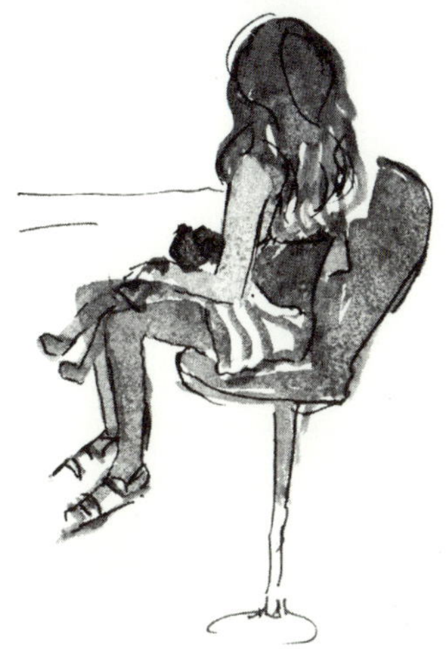

Child with doll: watercolour and pen, 4 × 2½ in (100 × 60 mm)

QUESTIONS AND ANSWERS

Question Can I learn to draw?

Answer Of course. If you can learn to write you can learn to draw. Some people will be able to draw better than others just as some people can write better. The key is practice, application and an interest in the subject. Inspiration and talent are more abstract and ephemeral, but the greatest artistic talent, like that of a musician, will falter without continuous practice.

Question Can I be creative with my work?

Answer Yes, of course you can, but first you must master the tools you use. The more skill you have with these the easier it is to be creative and to express yourself in an original way.

Question Should I use a broad or a fine pen nib?

Answer I prefer fine points such as the Stylo pens 0.25 to 0.35 for small drawings. Fibre and ball points have a variety of nib thicknesses so try them out first. Of the dip pens the Gillott 303 is the best pen, in my opinion, but there are many with finer nibs which are excellent, like the 290, 291 and 170, all supplied by Daler-Rowney.

Question What colours should I use?

Answer Limit your watercolour palette to about six colours at the most (see the chapter on equipment, page 8). I find tubes easier to carry. Watercolour pencils are useful but don't carry a large box when out sketching. There are some excellent Daler-Rowney coloured pencils, which you can buy in half lengths. Berol Prismacolor too is a good coloured pencil in strong colours and both these can be used with watercolour.

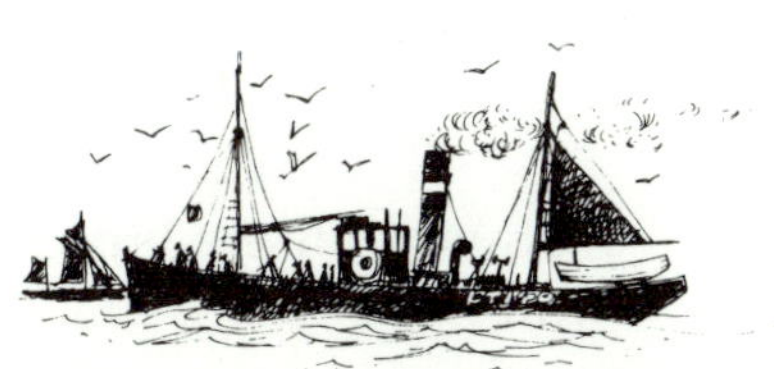

Steam trawler: technical pen, 2 × 4 in (50 × 100 mm)

Question Should I put people into architectural scenes?

Answer In an architectural or street scene, figures give a sense of scale and proportion to the drawing and bring it to life.

Question What sort of paper should I buy in sketchbooks?

Answer Thin cartridge, or even bank paper, is suitable in the small pocket sketchbooks. Ivorex board is excellent if you want a smoother hard surface. My favourite for sketching and watercolour is the Bockingford 140 lb sketch pad. A good-quality fine cartridge paper, such as the Frisk Gallery cartridge, is excellent for line, wash, pencil or pastel.

Question Should I use a quill or dip pen as well as a technical pen?

Answer The technical pens made by Rotring, Staedtler and Faber-Castell are extremely useful and easy to carry, but the Gillott nib with Indian ink gives a variety and sensitivity of line which cannot be achieved with other pens.

Question Should I outline a sketch first before using colour?

Answer Start direct with watercolour on to your paper or over a light pencil or crayon outline. This gives the work freshness and freedom. Strengthen later with a pen if needs be.

Question Can I use coloured paper for watercolour?

Answer Coloured paper, like that in the Daler-Rowney Ingres sketchbooks, is excellent and can be very effective when used for watercolour work, particularly if you add Chinese White or gouache on top. Gouache with added pen and ink gives a lively and fresh look to sketches.

Question Can I mix my media?

Answer Of course. Try to experiment with mixtures; for example, pen and watercolour; pencil, crayon and watercolour; pen and gouache; pastel, oil pastel and pen, and any other combination you fancy. Sketching is all about experimenting. And the more you experiment the more you learn.

Question Should I ask permission to draw someone?

Answer Most people do not really mind being drawn or having their houses drawn – in fact, they might even pay you for it afterwards! However, if you need to go on to private land, especially if it is farmland, then it is better to ask for permission. When abroad watch the local customs and religious taboos. Mostly artists are welcomed and often over-zealously watched, but in some Arab countries, for instance, people don't like being drawn or photographed, and even in places like New York, in the ethnic areas downtown, you have to be very careful. But when you respect local customs and try to talk to people they are usually only too friendly.

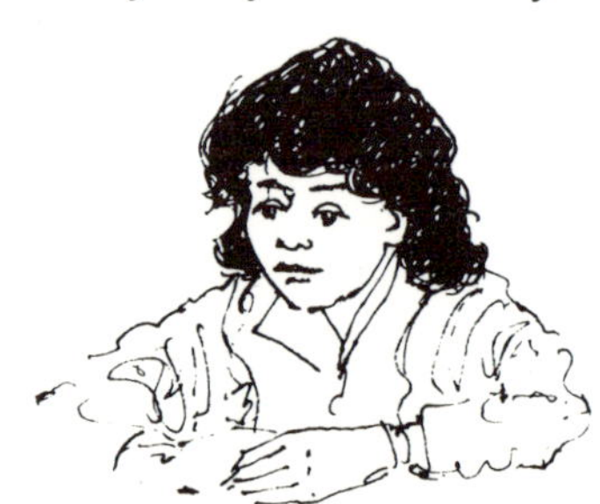

Girl seated: felt pen, s/s

Question Do I need architectural knowledge to draw buildings?

Answer I think that I have already dealt with this question in the text but the answer is that it certainly helps to have a basic knowledge. I have written a book about this, entitled *Drawing and Painting Buildings*, (Collins).

Question When should I stop working on a drawing?

Answer This is the $54,000 question. Generally, when you begin to think you should stop it is already too late. However, if you do not on occasion take your work too far, you will never know when to stop next time! With watercolours though, as a general rule you should avoid more than three washes over each other.

Question Should I always draw and paint quickly?

Answer Not necessarily. Some subjects need meticulous observation and careful drawing, others, like a group of moving animals, need a speedy execution.

Question Should I copy other artists' work?

Answer I have never benefited from slavishly copying another person's work, but I believe it has helped some artists. The danger is that your work gradually begins to look like the other person's work even when you are not copying. However, no harm can be done by trying out another artist's technique and eventually it should be incorporated into your own methods. We are all influenced by other artists to a certain extent, but a gradual development of one's own individual technique is most desirable. However, do make a point of studying the Old Masters in museums and galleries whenever you can as it can be a real inspiration, especially the sketchbooks of artists like Constable and Turner.

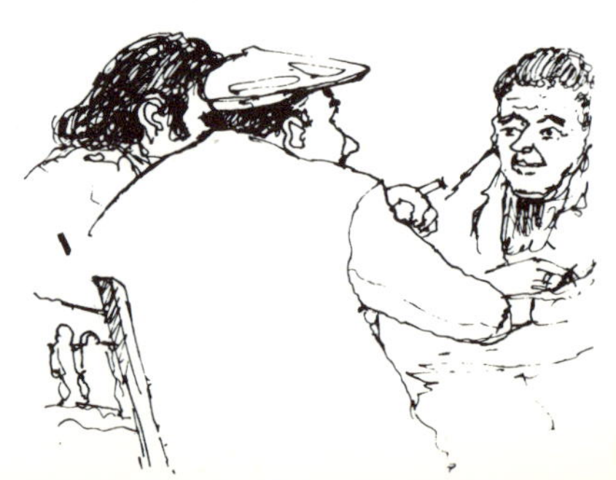

Argument: fibre tipped pen, 3 × 4 in (77 × 100 mm)

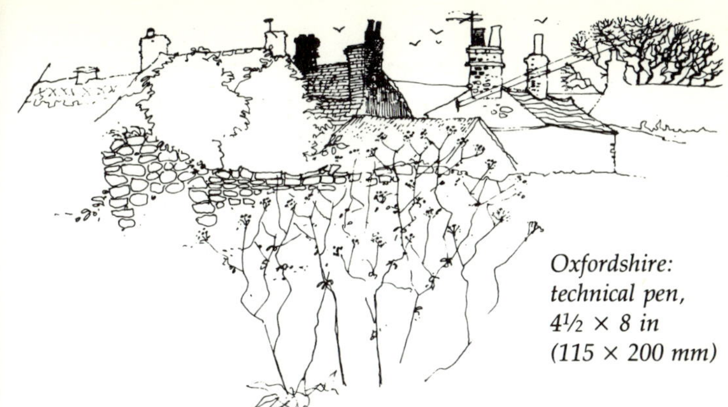

Oxfordshire: technical pen, 4½ × 8 in (115 × 200 mm)

Question Is the sky the lightest part of a painting?

Answer The answer is nearly always yes, but occasionally no, when a dark sky accentuates the whiteness of a building, for example, or certain highlights in the foreground are lighter than the sky.

Question What are the best rules to remember when sketching?

Answer Keep drawing whenever you can as it is by practice alone that you will turn yourself into a good artist. There is no short cut and the best rule is to draw every day even if it is only for a few minutes.

ACKNOWLEDGEMENTS

I would like to thank the following for permission to reproduce sketches on the pages specified: Royle Publications (pages 46 and 103); The Countryman (pages 57, 60 and 96); The Good Hotel Guide (page 107); and John Murray (page 111).

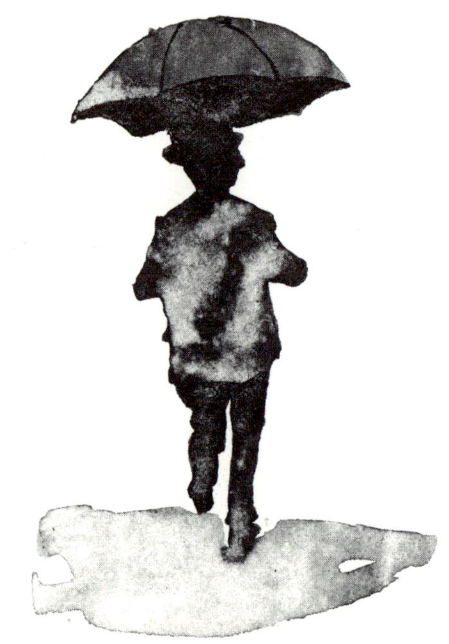

Crossing a Parisian street, watercolour, S/S